Sarasota Fishing Secrets

Tips, techniques, forecasts and detailed maps

Captain Jim Klopfer has been running fishing charters in Sarasota since 1991. He is sharing his extensive knowledge of the area along with angling techniques and fish habits.

Getting Started

The first thing any angler needs to start enjoying the sport of fishing is equipment. This is true of most hobbies and fishing is no exception. This basically consists of rods, reels, line, and terminal tackle as well as a few tools and other accessories.

RODS and REELS

Spinning tackle is the best choice for the majority of fishing situations than an angler will encounter. It is easy to use and a quality outfit can be purchased for around $150. Spincast gear (many of us started out with this, catching bluegill in ponds) just does not hold up in saltwater. Conventional or baitcasting tackle certainly has a place in saltwater fishing, particularly when using heavier lures and terminal tackle. But for most anglers, particularly those just getting into the sport, spinning tackle is the way to go.

Walking into a tackle store can be intimidating and overwhelming. But, it really isn't that complicated. A local bait and tackle shop will give an angler better advice and service than most "box" stores will. They will also have a good selection of tackle and lures that works well for that local area. The best all-around choice is a 7' medium action rod with a matching reel. There are many brands to choose from along with a wide range of prices. A $60 rod and $75 reel will work well for years with decent care. A 7' rod will allow and angler to fish structure such as bridges and docks and still be light enough to fish small lures and baits. My second choice would be a 6 ½' rod with a matching reel. This lighter outfit is better for casting jigs and smaller live baits. These two outfits will cover just about any inshore fishing situation.

LINES

There are many line choices out on the market, all have advantages and disadvantages. Monofilament line is the least expensive and the easiest for a novice angler to use. It has been used for many years and is a fine choice. Braided line has become very popular in recent years. It is more expensive but lasts a long time. Braid has almost no stretch and greater sensitivity, however line management is critical; snarls are difficult to remove. Also, knots are a little harder to tie with braid. In between are hybrid and fluorocarbon lines. These are kind of the best of both worlds and are also excellent choices, though a bit pricey. 10 to 12 pound monofilament or 20 pound braid would be the best choices.

TERMINAL TACKLE

Terminal tackle consists of the hook or lure that is tied onto the end of the line, along with any leader, weight, or swivels that might be used.

HOOKS and ARTIFICIAL LURES

Hooks come in many shapes, sizes and designs. For the vast majority of live and frozen bait situations, a 1/0 live bait hook will work quite well. If larger or smaller baits are used, the hook size should be changed accordingly. Anglers should match the hook to the size of the bait being used more than the size of the fish being targeted. A small hook will catch a large fish! Cut-offs from Spanish mackerel, bluefish, or other toothy critters will require a switch to a long shank hook. Some anglers prefer "circle hooks" and these are required for fishing the offshore reefs. Sizing is a bit different and when using then, the hook is not "set" but instead the line is just reeled tight while the rod tip is raised and the fish will hook itself.

There is probably nothing more confusing than artificial lures when it comes to fishing. There are endless choices of colors, sizes, and styles, but it can be simplified to some degree. Many anglers assume that live bait will always out-fish "fake" bait, but this is not always the case. There are situations where lures will out-produce live bait. The three basic types of lures used often here on the Suncoast are jigs, spoons, and plugs.

A jig is a simple lure that consists of a hook with a piece of lead molded into it. Some type of "tail" is then added and when worked properly imitates a baitfish or crustacean. Tails can be bucktail or synthetic hair or a plastic body. The plastic baits are very popular as they are relatively inexpensive and they can be easily changed. Jig heads in 1/8 ounce and 1/4 ounce are most popular. Gold, Glow, pearl, olive, red/copper, and chartreuse are all effective colors.

A spoon is a curved piece of metal with a hook in it; pretty simple but they catch fish! Silver and gold are the two most effective colors. Silver works best in clear water and gold is more productive in stained water. These lures can be cast a long way and are very easy to use. Weedless spoons are very effective in shallow water.

Plugs are plastic or wood lures that usually resemble a baitfish. They are very effective however they have a couple of drawbacks; they are fairly expensive and usually sport a pair of treble hooks making them potentially dangerous and also resulting in more damage to a fish that is to be released. There are very effective cast or trolled and account for some very large fish!

LEADERS

In most angling situations a leader will be required. This is sometimes called a "shock leader". Many of the species encountered in our area have sharp teeth and/or raspy gill plates. Tying the hook or lure directly to the line with result in a lot of lost fish. So, a short piece (18"-24") of leader is used. 30 pound is a good all-round choice but can be bumped up to 40 or 50 pound if larger fish are around or in stained water. Conversely, if the water is very clear, a move to 20 pound leader may be required. Flourocarbon leader is the best choice but inexpensive monofilament leader can also be used. Anglers should purchase several spools of different strengths. As a convenience, most shops offer pre-made rigs with hooks, swivels, and leader all tied up and ready to go.

SWIVELS AND WEIGHTS

The final pieces of terminal tackle are swivels and weights. A swivel can be used between the leader and main line and will greatly reduce line twist. It is crucial when using a spoon. Weights come in a variety of sized and shapes. Split shot are small weights which are pinched onto the line. Sliding sinkers knows as "egg sinkers" are popular and easy to use.

TOOLS and ACCESSORIES

Lastly, there are tools and accessories. Every angler will need a pair of pliers. Nail clippers can be handy for trimming knots. A landing net, bait bucket, filet knife, and a release tool (A MUST in my opinion) are other options. Now, let's go fishing!

FISHING WITH LIVE BAIT

Fishing with live bait will produce the most action for the majority of novice anglers. The two predominant baits used here on the West Coast of Florida are shrimp and baitfish. Shrimp can be purchased at most bait shops and are the "nightcrawler of saltwater", they catch everything! Anglers fishing from shore will need a bait bucket to keep them alive. Most buckets have holes in them so that the bucket can be lowered into the water, insuring a supply of fresh water to the shrimp. Small battery operated air pumps can be purchased to keep them frisky in a five gallon bucket. Most fishing boats have an aerated baitwell.

Baitfish come in all shapes and sizes; big fish have been eating small fish for a long time. The two basic types are "whitebait" such as scaled sardines (pilchards), threadfin herring, and sardines and "finfish" including pinfish and grunts. Fishing with baitfish is more complicated; they must be caught by the angler in most cases and are more difficult to keep alive. Whitebait in particular need the water changed constantly. Pinfish and grunts can be kept alive in a bucket for a while.

The rig for using live bait is fairly simple. A #10 black swivel is tied onto the end of the main line and 24" of 30 pound fluorocarbon leader is tied onto the other end of the swivel. A hook finishes off the rig. Hook choice is determined by the size of the bait being used. In most cases, a #1/0 short shank live bait hook is a good choice. Shrimp are hooked either under the horn just behind the eyes or in the tail. Baitfish can be hooked under the dorsal fin or through the lips or nose. A float can be used to suspend the bait from the bottom and weights can be added to both get the bait down to the bottom along with adding distance to the cast. Baits can also be "free-lined" which means just hooked on with no other weight and allowed to swim naturally in the current.

It is probably safe to say that over the years more trout and other species have been caught using a live shrimp under a popping cork than any other method. A popping cork is a float that has a concave face with a weight at the bottom. The float sits up-right in the water and when the rod tip it "twitched" sharply, the float makes a "pop" which imitates fish feeding on the surface and attracts gamefish to the bait. In recent years noisy "clacker" type floats have become popular. These are effective but one drawback if that the depth cannot be changed as easily since the leader is tied on versus the popping cork which slides onto the line.

Using the popping cork rig is quite easy. The cork is attached 3-4 feet above the hook, which is baited with a live shrimp. If a lot of current or wind exists, adding a small split shot a foot above the hook may be required to keep the bait down. A 7' rod works best as the rig is "lobbed" out using an easy swinging motion. Once the bait settles, reel up the slack and twitch the rod sharply. The cork will "pop" and the shrimp will jump up, and then slowly settle back down. Fish find this difficult to resist! Wait 30 seconds or so and repeat. Do this several times then reel it in and cast out to a different spot. When the float disappears, reel the slack up and set the hook. This works well from both the shore and from a drifting boat. A bait fish can also be used in place of a shrimp.

Both live shrimp and bait fish can be "free-lined". This simply consists of hooking the bait, casting it out to a likely spot, and waiting for it to get eaten. This works best over deeper grass flats, off the beach, and near structure such as docks and bridges. It will not be effective in shallow water as the bait will go down into the bottom to hide.

Bottom fishing is another popular method when using live bait. This is usually done from shore or from an anchored boat. The amount of weight needed will be determined by the depth of the water and the strength of the current. The rule of thumb is to use only enough weight to hold the bottom. If the bait moves too much it will eventually snag on the bottom. In shallow water a split shot or two will often times be enough. In deeper water or if current is present, a sliding egg sinker should be used. The sinker can be added on the main line above the swivel, this is called a "fish finder" rig. It allows the fish to pick up the bait and move without feeling the weight. Another method is the "knocker" rig which puts the weight right on the eye of the hook. This works well and will not hang up as often. Frozen bait and fresh cut bait can also be used effectively when bottom fishing.

FISHING WITH LURES

The main obstacle to overcome when using lures is confidence. Until an angler starts catching fish with them, they tend to doubt their effectiveness and want to switch back to live bait. But lures can often times catch more fish than bait. Their main advantage over bait is that they cover a LOT more water since they are always in motion. Also, lures can trigger strikes from fish that are not actively feeding. There is also the "hassle" factor, no need to purchase bait and keep it alive.

Jig heads come in many colors, but white and red are the two most popular. Tails also come in various shapes, sizes, and colors. Shad and curly tail baits imitate fish while paddle tail and shrimp bodies mimic crustaceans. Both catch plenty of fish. Don't get overwhelmed; just pick up a handful of heads in white and red in 1/8 and ¼ ounce along with some packages of bodies. A basic color selection of gold, white, red/rootbeer, and chartreuse in both bait and grub style will be all an angler needs to get started. One advantage of these types of jigs is the ease with which tails can be replaced and colors changed. They are also very economical. Scented soft plastic baits such as Gulp! are a bit more expensive, but on slow days they can make a big difference.

Jigs can also be purchased that are manufactured with nylon or natural fibers. Bucktail jigs have been around a long time and white is the best color. Spro jigs are a quality bucktail jig that is an excellent lure. Pompano jigs are usually made with artificial fibers. Typically, they have a heavy head and a short tail. A good example is the Bomber Saltwater Grade Pompano jig. I prefer the chrome head/green tail combo. While very productive, hair jigs are not as durable or cost effective as the jig/grub combo is. They are a great choice for pompano and speckled trout, but not for bluefish and mackerel.

Passes and inlets can be great spots to fish jigs, as long as the water is clean. Most passes have shallow bars and deep channels and fish can be in either of those spots. In the deeper water, vertically jigging while drifting with the tide is a time-proven technique for pompano and other species. Simply drop a jig to the bottom and drift along while sharply raising the rod tip every couple of seconds, then allow the bait to flutter back to the bottom. Heavier pompano style jigs work very well in this application. Each time the bait hits the bottom it will kick up a puff of sand, imitating a crab or other crustacean. On the shallow bars, casting jigs out and retrieving them back to the boat is the preferred method.

Jigs are very productive on the deep grass flats. Speckled trout in particular are suckers for a jig/grub combo, but bluefish, Spanish mackerel, pompano, cobia, flounder, sea bass, grouper, jacks, and ladyfish will all readily take a jig. The lure is cast out and retrieved back using a sharp "twitch", generally from the 10:00 to 12:00 position. Most bites occur as the jig is falling, seemingly helpless. Anglers who keep the line tight as the jig falls will detect more strikes. Darker colors such as olive and rootbeer work very well on the deep flats. Another popular technique is to fish a jig two feet under a noisy cork. The rig is cast out, allowed to settle, and the rod tip is sharply twitched. This causes the cork to make a loud noise, attracting fish. It also causes the jig to jerk up and then slowly settle back down. The cork not only keeps the lure from hanging in the grass, strikes are easily seen as it disappears.

Depending on weather conditions, fishing can be very good in the inshore Gulf of Mexico for both surf fisherman and anglers in boats. Good conditions would be clean, clear water in the mid-60s to mid-70's. Jigs cast from shore will catch pompano, whiting, jacks, mackerel, and ladyfish. Anglers fishing from boats will target surface activity from breaking false albacore and Spanish mackerel.

Spoons are both effective and very easy to use. They cast a mile and the retrieve is pretty simple; just reel it in and add a twitch now and again. Vary the speed until you find what the fish want that day. A swivel is required to eliminate line twist. Silver is the most popular color and works very well in clear water. Gold spoons work better in darker water over the flats and gold weedless spoons are a proven bait in very shallow water. Spoons are also very effective when trolled for mackerel and other species.

Plugs catch big fish. They are more expensive, the treble hooks require more care, and generally speaking they produce fewer strikes, but they catch big fish. Many of the largest snook have fallen prey to plugs, as have king and Spanish mackerel, cobia, big trout, reds, jacks, and more. Plugs come in two basic varieties; topwater and subsurface. Topwater plugs are most effective early and late in the day in fairly shallow water. Subsurface plugs will catch fish all day long. The size and shape of the lip will determine how deep it dives. Some plugs suspend and have no lip.

Topwater plugs come in two styles, poppers and "walk the dog" baits. Poppers are very easy to fish and are quite effective. The Rapala Skitter-Pop, Rebel Pop-R, and Chug-Bug are three popular examples. These are floating baits that have a concave face. The technique is simple; cast it out, let it settle for a moment, then twitch the rod tip sharply causing the face of the plug to dig into the water and make a loud "pop". The famous Zara Spook is the best known example of a "walk-the-dog" lure, but the Raplala Skitterwalk and MirrOlure Top Dog are also local favorites. The retrieve is a bit more difficult to master. After being cast out, the rod tip is held down near the surface and a rhythmic twitching retrieve causes the lure to dance back and forth on the surface.

One common mistake anglers make is working topwater baits too quickly and aggressively. This is particularly true on a very calm day. Slow, subtle action will generally draw more strikes. Another mistake often made is striking took soon. The sight of a large predator blowing up on a topwater plug is very exciting, often resulting in a reflex strike that pulls the lure out of the fish's mouth. Instead, wait until the weight of the fish is felt and set the hook in a smooth, sideways manner. This is safer as well.

While a topwater strike can be spectacular, more fish are caught on sub-surface baits. Most of these lures float on the surface and dive down when retrieved. Primarily, the lip on the lure determines the depth that the plug will run, however line size and speed are also other factors. Most lure manufacturers will have the pertinent information on the box. Rapala X-Raps are my personal favorites. They are available in a wide variety of colors and sizes. Generally speaking, lures that dive down two to five feet are the most effective in our local waters. Match the size of the plug to the available forage. Olive is my favorite all around color, but gold/black and chartreuse work great in stained water and pearl and silver are very effective in clear water.

Suspending plugs such as the venerable MirrOlure can be deadly, particularly on speckled trout. They sink slowly and are worked back in a twitch-and-pause retrieve. That "pause", where the bait just suspends, seemingly helpless, really triggers strikes. Lipless crankbaits such as the Rattletrap are very easy to use; just cast it out and reel it back in, they have a great built-in action. Chrome with a blue back is the favorite color.

Plugs are versatile; just about every gamefish that inhabits the Suncoast will devour them. In addition to casting to structure for snook, redfish, jacks, and other species, plugs are deadly when fished over the grass flats. On a recent charter I had a pair of eleven year old boys score on a mess of Spanish mackerel using an olive size (08) X-Rap. They cast into the thick bait schools near Big Pass and burned the baits back as fast as they could turn the reel handle. Needless to say, the strikes were explosive!

Plugs also catch a lot of speckled trout, often times fooling larger than average sized fish. Topwater baits are an excellent choice for fishing very shallow water early and late in the day. In late summer shallow bars on the edge of grass flats load up with bait, which in turn attracts gamefish. Add in a high tide at first light and the result is an excellent situation to catch a nice fish on topwater!

Suspending plugs such as the MirrOlure are deadly on speckled trout fished over the deeper grass, from four to eight feet of water. They also fool mackerel, bluefish, jacks, and other species. These baits do not have a lip; therefore they do not "dive". Instead, they are cast out and allowed to sink for several seconds, then twitched sharply. The lure just hangs there motionless, helpless, inducing a fish to strike it.

Trolling plugs is a great technique to locate fish when scattered about in a large area. It is also works well with children and novice anglers; if they can hold a rod, they can catch a fish. This applies to the inshore bays, passes, and Gulf of Mexico. The #8 olive saltwater X-Rap is my "Go to" lure for trolling. Simply let out about half the line out, close the bail, and drive the boat around just a bit above idle speed. Sometimes working the rod tip will elicit more strikes. One trick that serves me well is to troll in the passes. The traditional method is to drift with the current and cast jigs, plugs, or spoons. Once the drift is complete, the boat is idles back up and the drift repeated. Since you are easing along nice and slow, why not drag a plug behind? Many mornings I catch more Spanish mackerel this way as they prefer fast moving baits.

Casting and trolling plugs in the inshore Gulf of Mexico is an extremely effective technique in the spring and again in the fall when pelagic species move through. A large Yozuri 3D will produce some very nice king mackerel and large Spanish mackerel. Look for birds and bait schools on the surface and troll around the edges of the bait, not right through the middle. The inshore reefs off of Lido Key hold a LOT of fish and are very reliable producers.

Sight casting to "breaking" fish is terrific sport. Spanish mackerel and false albacore (bonita, little tunny) will often be seen tearing up schools of helpless baitfish on the surface. The Spanish will stay up on top longer and not move as much as the false albacore. With either species, ease into position and cast into the fish or troll around the edge of them and be prepared to hear your drag scream! Anglers can also employ the same tactics from the beach to catch Spanish mackerel.

Techniques and Tactics

DEEP GRASS FLATS

There are several approaches that can be successfully employed on the deep flats. The first choice to make is whether to anchor or drift the flats. Large expanses are most efficiently fished by drifting while smaller patches or edges are best fished from an anchored boat. Working the edge of a shallow flat that drops off sharply into deeper water is a deadly technique that is particularly effective on low tides. The fish will tend to stage on the edge as there isn't enough water up on top of the flat. While artificial lures can be used this is a situation that is best suited for live bait. A live shrimp or small baitfish free-lined over the edge is simple and very effective.

Drifting the flat while casting lures is an extremely popular and effective technique. One benefit of using artificial lures is that anglers can cover a lot of water fairly quickly. This is important on the larger expanses of grass; the sooner the fish are located, the better! The primary lure used on the Gulf Coast of Florida is the lead head jig and grub combo. This versatile and inexpensive bait will catch anything that swims and has resulted in many a tasty fish dinner. Jigs come in a variety of sizes and colors but ¼ ounce heads in white or red are all that is required. Plastic bodies also come in a myriad of shapes and colors but again it does not need to be complicated. A selection of gold, pearl, olive, rootbeer, and charteuse bodies in both the shad tail and flat grub tail will cover most situations. Scented soft plastics such as Gulp! Shrimp can make the difference if the bite is slow.

Hard plugs also catch a lot of fish. The venerable suspending MirrOlure baits have been a staple in tackle boxes for decades. They slowly sink and when twitched suspend motionless in the water. Speckled trout in particular find them irresistible. Shallow diving plugs such as the Rapala X-Rap also work well when retrieved erratically. They are a great choice when surface activity is present and are also effective when trolled.

Live bait can certainly be used while drifting as well. In fact, it is a fair bet that more speckled trout have been put on ice using a live shrimp under a popping cork than any other method. This is simply a #1/0 live bait hook with a "popping cork" placed on the line three feet or so above the hook. A live shrimp is hooked under the horn and the rig is cast out in front of the boat as it drifts along. The cork has a concave face that "pops" when twitched sharply. This simulates the sound of feeding fish and will attract trout and other species to the shrimp which is dangling there helplessly. There are also several manufacturers of noisy floats such as the Cajun Thunder float. These are very noisy and can be cast a long way. The cork is tied on to the running line and then a leader connects the cork to the hook. Popping corks work great in water depths of six feet or less. A live shrimp can even be replaced with a light jig or artificial shrimp. Live baits can also be drifted out behind the boat. This works well in deeper water and under breezy conditions.

Live baitfish are another terrific producer on the flats. Pinfish and grunts can be purchased at local bait shops or caught out on the flats and are best fished under a float to keep them from getting in the grass. "Whitebait" is a local term used to describe the schools of small silver bait fish that cover the flats in the warmer months. Scaled sardines (also known as pilchards) and threadfins (greenies) are the two most prolific species. Pilchards are the preferred bait as they are much hardier than the threadies, but both are equally effective. Baitfish are sighted on the grass or chummed into range and then cast netted and quickly put into a large, well aerated baitwell. Jack mackerel or canned cat food mixed with bread is a popular chum as well as bulk tropical fish food.

In the summertime these baitfish are thick on the shallow grass near the passes. Loading up the live well with bait practically guarantees success. Once the bait is acquired, anchor up-current of a flat and toss out a handful of bait. Repeat this every few minutes and if the fish are there they will show up in short order. Once the action heats up, slow down the chum flow; use just enough to keep them excited. I average one hundred fish mornings all summer long using this method.

As with all fishing techniques there are subtle nuances which will increase success. Here are some tips that will help your trips be more successful:

1) Choose a flat that has the wind and current moving in the same direction. Boat positioning and bait presentation will be better. This holds true both when drifting and anchoring.

2) When drifting, keep an anchor with 20' of line tied off. Once fish are located, quietly slide the anchor in and work that area thoroughly. When the action slows, pull the anchor and continue the drift.

3) Try and set up a drift that covers different depths on the flat. Drifting from eight feet of water into four feet of water is better than drifting at one depth.

4) Keep the noise down. Have the landing net out and keep the bait well lid open. Slamming hatches will shut down the fish!

SHALLOW FLATS

It sounds like a contradiction, but often times the larger fish are in shallower water. But these fish are spooky in skinny water and did not get that old by being reckless. Shallow water fishing is a "quality over quantity" situation, anglers who choose to fish this way need to be patient. Artificial lures are used most often, it is difficult fishing live bait in very shallow water. However a live pilchard or large live shrimp can be extremely effective fished under a small float.

Jigs, plugs, and spoons are all good choices when fishing the shallow grass. A gold weedless spoon is an old-school bait that remains effective today. It can be cast a long way, is relatively weedless, and redfish in particular love them! Jigs can work well though the angler needs to go lighter, down to a 1/16 ounce jig head. Plug caster are pretty much limited to topwater plugs as diving plugs will foul on the grass.

Although fish may be encountered anywhere on the flats, certain areas will consistently hold more fish. Oyster bars, potholes (small depressions in the shallow grass) and mangrove shorelines with slightly deeper water are all likely spots. Look for flats with "life" on it; baitfish, mullet schools, and bird life. Stealth and patience are required as you try and sneak up on the fish. Sometimes you will actually see the fish, but most of the bites will come blind casting. Waders will score as they really reduce the disturbance in the water.

Fish love structure, it is an undeniable fact. It provides cover and attracts forage. All species of fish can be taken around structure, but the primary targets will be sheepshead, snapper, flounder, gag grouper, redfish, snook, jack crevelle, and black drum. Sheepshead are very reliable in winter and early spring and they will often times bite when the water is cold and dirty and other species shut down. Mangrove snapper school up on the channel edges and bridges in the summer time. Snook, reds, and jacks are available all year.

Structure takes many forms; bridges, docks, seawalls, rip-rap, rock piles, artificial reefs, oyster bars, and holes. Passes are generally filled with fish-holding structure. Docks and oyster bars are abundant in our area, along with several bridges.

Deep Water Structure:

In most instances, a vertical presentation is the most effective way to target fish in deeper water. A knocker rig works very well in this presentation. It is simply a sliding sinker that rests up against the hook. This results in the bait resting right on the bottom and allows a fish to move off with the bait without detecting any weight. A two foot piece of heavier leader helps prevent cut-offs on the sharp rocks. The baited hook is lowered and allowed to lie on the bottom with a taught line. As with all structure fishing, use as little weight as possible, just enough to hold the bottom. The best time to fish deeper areas is during periods of slow tidal movement as a lot of current makes fishing too difficult.

Shallow Water Structure:

Docks and bridge pilings in four to twelve feet of water make up the majority of structure in Florida waters. Anchoring several boat lengths up current and tossing the bait back towards the structure is the best approach when fishing these spots. Whenever possible, use a minimal rig consisting of a two foot piece of leader, a hook, and a split shot. If heavy current exists, use the "knocker rig" with a light weight. When the water in the passes is clean, docks adjacent to the passes will be productive. After a front moves through, the passes will be full of cold, dirty water. Residential canals and other protected areas will offer better fishing as most species prefer cleaner water.

Do not overlook oyster bars as structure! Any bar that has a drop off into three or four feet of water may hold snook, reds, sheepshead, jack crevelle, and other species. Quietly approach the bar and anchor as far away as possible to avoid spooking fish. Free lining a live shrimp or pilchard with no weight is the most productive technique when fishing shallow bars. A low, incoming tide is normally the best time to target these fish-holding structures. Fish will stage in the deeper water waiting until the tide floods and they can get up on top of the bar. Once that occurs, they scatter out and are more difficult to locate.

The coldest weather will send fish scampering into creeks and canals. The water will be warmer, which also attracts bait fish. Deep holes will hold fish, especially on the low tide stages. Holes and changes in depths are often overlooked by other anglers. Treat these spots just like and other structure, anchor up-current and let the bait flow back naturally either free-lined or with a split shot.

ARTICLES

Here are some articles that Captain Jim has written over the years. Some of the information is repetitive.

Winter Tactics

It was difficult to tell whether a fish was making the rod tip move or whether it was my angler shivering. That question was answered when the rod bowed over and line began peeling off of the reel. The cold certainly wasn't affecting the sheepshead that felt the sting of the hook in its mouth. After a brief tug-of-war, the fish tired and came alongside the boat for a quick photograph. All of a sudden, my happy angler was no longer cold!

Contrary to popular belief, January is winter, even in Florida, and it does get cold. To be successful, anglers need to adapt to the different conditions that are presented this time of year. First, let's go through the weekly weather cycle. It begins after a cold front moves through. The wind will be out of the north east and it will be chilly in the morning. The next couple of days will be pleasant and sunny with east winds. As the next front approaches, the wind will shift south with clouds and a chance of rain before the front moves through and it blows hard out of the northwest. The best days are usually the ones with south winds, just before the front moves through and the pressure is just starting to drop.

Tides are also a factor in January. Morning tides can be extremely low, especially when coupled with a northeast wind. This will congregate fish in holes and deep channels, there simply is not enough water on the flats for fish to be comfortable. Holes in creeks and canals will produce sheepshead, redfish, snook, trout, drum, and flounder on the low tide stages. Afternoons will often be more productive as the day warms and the tide rises, especially for speckled trout. Passes and the surrounding flats will be productive several days after a front passes as the water clears, fish do not like dirty water. Backwater areas away from the passes that offer deep grass flats, oyster bars, bridges, creeks, and canals will be more productive immediately after the front. Water quality is usually better as it is protected from dirty water that comes in for the Gulf of Mexico.

Shrimp are extremely effective baits this time of year. Cold water temperatures will result in fish being more lethargic. A live or freshly dead shrimp fished on the bottom with catch just about every species. Frozen shrimp are a good second choice. On lower tide stages, deeper areas will be more productive. Oyster bars that drop off sharply, deeper holes in creeks and canals, bridges, docks, and channel edges are all good spots to try. A #1/0 hook on a 2' piece of 20 lb. leader with a split shot (if necessary) is all that is needed. If the action is slow, try chopping up a shrimp or two and tossing the pieces into the water, this may get the fish going. A live shrimp fished under a popping cork will catch a lot of speckled trout when fished over grass flats on a high tide.

Artificial lures will also catch plenty of fish in January. A jig/grub combo is perhaps the most popular and effective lure. Bouncing a jig down channel edges and in both passes will produce pompano, trout, ladyfish, and other species. Again, in cold water a subtle retrieve will usually elicit more strikes. Sometimes tipping the jig (adding a tiny piece of shrimp) will make a big difference. Jigs will also fool speckled trout, pompano, and ladyfish on the deep grass flats. Darker colors such as olive and rootbeer are quite effective fished on a ¼ ounce jig head.

   Plugs are also effective winter baits. Suspending plugs such as the MirrOlure MirrOdine and 52 Series are deadly in cooler water. The lure is cast out, allowed to sing several seconds, and twitched sharply. The bait suspends there, seemingly helpless, triggering strikes. Snook and jack crevelle will migrate up into the many creeks and canals in our area. Shallow diving plugs such as the Rapala X-Rap series are very productive lures, allowing anglers to cover a lot of water fairly quickly. Olive and gold are two very productive colors.

   Take what Mother Nature gives you this month. Enjoy the warm, sunny days and fish the open flats. On cold, breezy days, don't fight it. Find a protected spot to hide and soak a shrimp on the bottom. Plenty of fish can be caught. I had a charter last January that sticks in my mind. The weather was awful, northwest winds at 20 + knots. I never put the boat on plane and we caught a ton of fish! We started off in the Intracoastal, catching sheepshead on live shrimp. Then, we located a school of ladyfish in a deep hole in a canal and caught one on every cast on rootbeer jigs. We finished up catching snook and jack crevelle on Rapala way up in Phillippi Creek. Be flexible and have fun this month while other less adventurous anglers stay at home.

Inshore Gulf Strategies

In the spring time and again in the fall, the entire west coast is blessed with fantastic light tackle fishing in the inshore Gulf of Mexico. This truly is world class fishing. Huge schools of bait fish will move through on their annual migrations, and the game fish are hot on their trail. While the primary species are king and Spanish mackerel, along with false albacore, other pelagics such as cobia, tarpon, and sharks will also be encountered. Optimum conditions are water temperature between 65 and 75 degrees, along with easterly breezes and clear water. This offers anglers with small boats an opportunity to catch large fish quite close to shore.

Several techniques are used in pursuit of these nomadic speedsters. The most exciting, when conditions dictate, is sight casting to "breaking" fish. A spinning rod with ten to twelve pound line is ideal and a reel with a smooth drag is essential. Casting rods can be used, although the light lures and baits make spinning outfits a better choice for most anglers. Small plugs such as a Rapala X-Rap are extremely effective baits that result in a high hook-up rate. Spoons, Diamond jigs, Gotchas, and jigs with bait tails will also catch plenty of fish. White and silver are the preferred colors. Be careful not to use lures that are too big, the forage is usually quite small, better to "match the hatch". A 24" piece of fluorocarbon shock leader is needed, start out with 20 lb in clear water and go up to 40 lb if cut-offs from mackerel become an issue.

A patient angler will prevail in this situation. Charging around from school to school will only result in putting the fish down. Instead, sit and wait for a good opportunity. A trolling motor is a great asset, allowing the angler to fine tune the boat's position. As with all fishing, vary baits and retrieves until a productive pattern is identified. The fish are usually quite aggressive and a fast, erratic retrieve will result in bone-jarring strikes.

This is a terrific situation to catch a nice fish on a fly rod. Long casts are not normally required and the fish are hungry and cooperative. An average sized little tunny will get deep into the backing on its initial run. As with spin fishing, try different retrieves and flies. Allowing the fly to settle a moment, then retrieving it back in with short, hard strips is often productive, while at other times just letting the fly sink through the bait, seemingly helpless, will trigger a strike.

Trolling is an extremely effective technique that will usually put more fish in the boat than sight casting. This can be particularly true on mornings when there is a chop on the surface, when the fish are not showing, or when targeting king mackerel. Plugs and spoons are the two most productive lures. Both lures can be trolled using a light trolling sinker or behind a planer, but a plug with a large lip will "trip" the planer. Shallow and deeper running plugs are effective on all species. Spinning and conventional rods are both fine for trolling plugs. Simply tie the lure to a 6' piece of 80 lb. fluorocarbon. Rapala X-Raps, Yozuri 3 D Minnows, and gold Bombers are all effective plugs.

The key to trolling several lures without tangling them is to vary the depth and distance that the lure is let out behind the boat. I use a "count back" method. The shallowest running bait is let out first with the engine idling in gear. This is usually a plug but can also be a spoon/trolling sinker combo. Count out to twenty five and then put the rod in an outside rod holder. Next shallowest would be the #1 planer. Count out to twenty while letting the line out. Put that rod on the other side of the boat. Last, and deepest, is the #2 planer or deep diving plug. Count out to fifteen and set the rod in a holder as close to center as possible. Now there are three baits at different depths and distances, allowing the boat to be turned without the lines fouling. Increase speed to four to five knots and troll while looking for birds, bait, and surface activity. Keeping the boat moving after a strike can result in multiple hook-ups.

While I prefer the excitement of tossing artificial lures and flies, drifting and slow trolling live bait will often out fish all other methods, and will usually catch the largest fish. Live shrimp and small baitfish that can be cast-netted up are best free lined on light tackle using a 2/0 long shank hook on a 24" piece of 30 lb. leader. This works great for catching Spanish mackerel and false albacore. Larger species such as king mackerel, cobia, tarpon, and sharks prefer a large threadfin or blue runner. Cast out a Sabiki rig into the bait pods and use a slight jigging motion to attract the bait. Once procured, use a heavy spinning rod (tarpon tackle is perfect for this) with a 5' piece of 80 lb. fluorocarbon leader and a 6/0 live bait hook. Drift the bait out behind the boat, a cork may be required if the wind and tide are slack.

Live baitfish can also be slow trolled. This is an extremely effective tactic for large kingfish. A "stinger" rig is preferred. This consists of a long wire leader with two hooks about 6" apart. The bait is attached by the nose to the first hook, the second hook swings free. The bait is let out 100 feet behind the boat and slowly trolled around the edges of bait schools and over structure. The boat should be in idle and moving as slowly as possible. Drags are set lightly allowing the fish to run after a strike. In most instances, the fish will be hooked in the side of the face with the stinger hook, necessitating the light drag pressure.

A couple of seasons back, I was out on the beach on a charter the day before Thanksgiving. It was a little choppy and the fish were not showing, so I had my clients drifting live baits out behind the boat. We had landed a small king and several nice Spanish mackerel when a rod baited with a big threadfin doubled over. Line peeled off the reel as my client scrambled to get the rod out of the holder. His face lit up as a hundred pounds of silver fury leapt several feet out of the water. Yes, a tarpon at the end of November! You never know what you might hook into off of the Suncoast beaches. Come and experience our Beach Bonanza for yourself!

Planers are deadly, but require the use of heavier tackle. A #1 planer on a 15-20 lb. conventional outfit and 20 feet of 50 lb. leader and will dive down six to eight feet at five knots. A #2 planer on a 30-40 lb. conventional rod and 20' of 80 lb. leader will work the 12'-15' depths. Match the spoon to the size of the planer. A 2"-3" Clark spoon works best on a #1 planer while a large King spoon works better on the #2 planer. Quality swivels on both ends of the leader will minimize line twist.

Fly casters will do well with an eight or nine weight rod with either a floating or intermediate sink tip line. The leader consists of an eight foot piece of 20 lb. fluorocarbon. Fly selection is easy, any small white fly will produce, my preference being a #4 white D.T. Special or Glass Minnow. A short piece of light wire will help with lost flies but will also result in fewer strikes. Large arbor fly reels with good drag systems and plenty of backing are required to catch false albacore.

Artificial reefs are plentiful throughout the area and are fish magnets. They are great places to start on days when the fish are not breaking on the surface. The same techniques will work, just be alert when trolling as the boats will usually be congregated over the reefs. Anglers can also anchor up and bottom fish for grouper, snapper, sheepshead, flounder, Key West grunts, triggerfish, and other species. A knocker rig works best to minimize snags.

Tarpon Fishing

The silence of the pre-dawn morning was broken by the sound of several large tarpon rolling gently on the surface. As guide eased the boat into range the angler made ready to cast. Several anxious moments passed before the fish showed themselves again. A crab was tossed out just ahead of the school; a perfect cast! It slowly sank for several seconds before the line got taut and moved off to the side. The angler reeled fast and hard as line screamed off the drag. One hundred pounds of silver fury cleared the surface by several feet, shaking its head violently and throwing the hook. Disappointment quickly turned to admiration; what a gallant fish!

That is a commonly played out scenario off of Sarasota beaches from May through July. This is truly world class angling. Very few places offer the opportunity to sight cast to fish this large using spinning or fly tackle. Many more tarpon are hooked than are actually landed. In fact, most Sarasota guides put more emphasis on stalking and hooking these behemoths than in actually landing them.

The fish generally show up in early May and are here in significant numbers by the third week in May. Early in the season the schools can be huge, numbering in the hundreds. Later in the season they break up into smaller "pods". By late July the fish have thinned out considerably, but so has the fishing pressure. Fish late in the year don't "show" as well but they bite better.

The technique is pretty straightforward. Get out on the beach before first light and sit a hundred yards or so from shore. Sit patiently while scanning the surface for fish. Once a school is sighted, an electric trolling motor is used to position the boat so that it intercepts the fish. The ideal situation would be a long cast up-wind of the school. The baits are cast out in front of the fish and hopefully a hook-up ensues. Anglers in larger boats can catch tarpon, but it is more difficult as they must anticipate where the fish might be and drift in front of them.

Heavy spinning tackle spooled with 25-30 pound line is the best choice for most anglers. Although the fish are very large, the baits are light. Conventional outfits can be used to drift baits out behind the boat but are not very practical for casting. The rig is pretty basic; double six feet of the running line using a Spider Hitch or Bimini Twist, then add 3 feet of 80 lb. leader using a Double Uni-Knot. Tie on a 5/0 live bait hook or large circle hook. A 3" crab is perfect and is hooked on the outer edges of the "point". Live bait fish such as pinfish, sardines, cigar minnows, threadfin herring, and blue runners are also productive and can be caught using a Sabiki rig.

Patience is required when tarpon fishing. It is very easy to get excited and overly aggressive. The angler who takes the time to get into perfect position will score more often than the impatient one who runs around. A couple words regarding etiquette; do NOT run an outboard near a school of tarpon! It is better to let them go, motor around and reposition than to fire up the "big motor" in a school of fish. Also, if another boat is working a school, leave them to it unless they wave you in. This is especially true in regards to fly fishing, give those guys plenty of room to work.

Winter Creek and River Fishing

Finding fish in January can be tough, especially after a cold front that has the water temperature around 50 degrees. Cold water will send fish scurrying for deep water. It will also send them back into creeks, rivers, and residential canals. The water can be as much as ten degrees warmer in the back end of canals. I have found that working these creeks and canals to be a very reliable winter pattern in Sarasota.

The best creeks and canals will have varying depths with some deeper water (6'-10'), along with cover such as mangroves, oyster bars, and docks. These will hold a variety of species including snook, redfish, sheepshead, speckled trout, black drum, jack crevelle, flounder, ladyfish, and even juvenile tarpon.

Live shrimp are extremely effective in this situation. Fish activity has slowed down and so will the successful angler. One of the best situations is to fish a deep hole in a creek on a low, incoming tide. The low water will congregate fish in the hole; it can literally be "fish in a barrel". A live shrimp hooked on a #1/0 live bait hook with a short piece of 30 lb shock leader and just enough split shot to get the bait to sink slowly to the bottom is the simple, but effective rig to use. Be patient and allow the scent to permeate the area, again, these fish will be bit more lethargic. A few pieces of diced up shrimp tossed into the water as chum will often times get the bite going.

Artificial lures can be very productive, too, and they offer the advantage of allowing an angler to cover a lot more water than when using live bait. The best technique is to drift with the tide while casting to likely looking structure such as docks and mangrove shorelines. Often times the fish will be right out in the middle "sunning" themselves, so cover the area thoroughly. I find that this pattern works best later in the day when the tide is coming in and the water has warmed up a bit.

Shallow diving plugs such as the Rapala X-Rap are my personal favorite lure to use in this application. My clients have caught some big snook and jacks using this technique. Simply cast it out and twitch the rod tip sharply and the lure will dive down several feet. Pause a moment, then repeat. Often times the strike will come as the bait sits there motionless. These lures can also deadly while trolled, so as you idle along let one out a hundred feet behind the boat. I have fooled many a big jack crevelle when trolling Rapalas!

Soft plastic baits work very well, too. Scented lures such as Gulp! have the advantages of both lures and bait. Darker colors such as rootbeer and "golden bream" seem to produce the best, and a contrasting white or chartreuse tail can sometimes help, too. Slowly bouncing the bait along the bottom will usually produce the most fish. These lures will catch more species than plugs will.

There are several rivers within a short drive of Sarasota that offer visitors a unique angling experience. The Manatee River, Braden River, Myakka River, and Peace River are all great places to fish for snook in the winter. The scenery is spectacular and the fishing can be fantastic. It is a "quality over quantity" situation; there will be times when there are not a lot of fish caught, but on every trip there is the chance to catch a trophy snook on fairly light tackle.

Creeks have saved the day for me on numerous occasions when the weather was less than ideal. One trip in particular comes to mind. I met my clients at CB's Saltwater Outfitters around noon and it was cold and windy. We almost cancelled the trip but decided to grab some live shrimp and give it a try. As we idled north, I knew that I needed to find a protected spot to fish, so I ducked into Phillippi Creek and anchored up on the edge of a five feet deep hole. I baited up both rods with live shrimp and cut up a couple more and tossed the chum into the hole. The first bait wasn't in the water for a minute when line stated screaming off the reel! It turned out to be a four pound sheepshead and we caught another dozen sheepies of varying sizes along with a couple of redfish.

The action slowed and I pulled the anchor. We drifted up the creek casting plugs and my clients caught several snook between 18" and 24" along with a pair of five pound jacks. It was a great trip that nearly did not happen. Once again, Phillippi Creek saved the day.

Summer Snookin'

There is little doubt that snook are the premier light tackle inshore fish in our region of Florida. These predators are the perfect game fish. They strike artificial lures and flies, leap clear out of the water, and are aggressive, yet challenging. I tell my clients that snook are very similar to largemouth bass in habit but with the muscle and attitude of a saltwater fish. They have a very large mouth which allows them to inhale their prey and are almost always found near structure. Snook can be very active or infuriatingly fussy.

August is a great month to target snook in the Sarasota area as there are multiple patterns and techniques that are productive. Snook spawn out on the beaches in the summer and there will still be fish out there in the surf. Passes will also hold concentrations of fish. Big Sarasota Pass on the north end of Siesta Key has abundant structure and deep water, making for prime snook habitat. Mangrove shorelines, oyster bars, docks, and bridges will also attract fish. Any spot that has a depth change, cover, current, and bait is likely to produce, particularly those close to the passes.

Artificial lures and live bait are both effective on snook. The choice really depends on angler preference and conditions. Personally, I LOVE plug fishing! I find that making a good cast right up against the mangroves and anticipating a snook attacking it as I twitch it through the strike zone to be very enjoyable. I prefer Rapalas, with the X-Rap being my favorite. Nothing beats a surface strike; topwater plugs such as the Zara Spook and Skitter Prop are proven baits.

Soft plastic baits are both versatile and extremely effective. The D.O.A. CAL series of baits is quite popular in this area. I like dark colors such as rootbeer and golden bream, especially after a bit of rainfall. A 1/8 ounce white head works well in shallow water and offers a contrast to the dark body. Heavier jig heads will be required in deeper water. When conditions are tough, scented baits can really make a big difference. Trigger-X and Gulp! both offer a good selection of quality lures.

Live bait catches fish; it is that simple, especially in the daytime. A large pilchard is tough to beat, but pinfish, grunts, and large shrimp also catch plenty of snook. Netting up a bunch of pilchards and using them to chum the fish into a feeding frenzy is a time-proven technique. Free lining baits under docks or along likely-looking shorelines is also productive. In shallow water a float will keep the bait from getting into the grass. Sometimes acquiring large pilchards can be difficult, especially in the summertime. However, 3" pinfish are abundant and are a good alternative. They also seem to catch larger fish.

The equipment and rig is the same with both live and artificial baits. A 7' rod and spinning reel spooled with braid or monofilament line is a good all-round choice. A 24" section of 30 lb fluorocarbon leader is attached to the running line, then the lure or a 1/0 live bait hook is tied on. I do not like to use swivels or other hardware. I prefer to double three feet of the running line using a Spider Hitch and attach the leader using a double uni-knot. I then tie on the hook or lure using a uni-knot.

Anglers looking for numbers of fish will do well fishing lighted docks and bridges after dark. Snook are nocturnal feeders and will be active after the sun sets. Lights attract shrimp and glass minnows, which in turn attracts the gamefish. Anchoring a long cast up-current from the light and casting into the shadow line is the preferred technique. D.O.A. shrimp, jigs, flies, plugs, and live shrimp will all produce....or not. Snook can be notoriously finicky! Night fishing also gives anglers a respite from the summer sun, just be mindful of thunderstorms.

Sarasota offers anglers a unique opportunity; sight casting to large snook on the beach. And the best part is that not only is a boat not required, it is actually a hindrance! Snook gang up on area beaches to spawn in the summertime. These fish will often be seen inches from the surf line. Small white bucktail jigs and flies are very productive, but plugs, spoons, and live bait will also fool their share of fish. Ideal conditions are clear water, little or no chop, an incoming tide, and an east wind. West winds churn up the water making sight fishing difficult. Snook will still bite for anglers blind casting around rocks and other structure. Point of Rocks on Siesta Key is a terrific spot to fish!

The technique is pretty straight-forward. Walking north will keep the sun to the rear, making the fish easier to spot. Stay ten feet or so from the surf, the added elevation will also assist in seeing snook. Once spotted, determine the direction that the fish are moving, and cast out in front of them. Light lures and flies will produce more bites.

The Best of Both Worlds

It is June and I have a morning charter. I also have a dilemma. The water temperature is in the mid-80s and the bay is full of bait fish. Artificial lures can be effective but live bait is tough to beat. Also, the idea of using the early morning "prime time" to catch bait is not appealing. So, what to do? Simple; take advantage of the first light bite by casting lures and mid-morning when things slow down a bit, fill the well with bait and use it to get the fish cranked back up!

This is a strategy that I use on my charters all summer long. There is often so much bait on the flats, particularly those flats near the passes where I often fish, that the speckled trout and other species can be difficult to fool on a lure. The exceptions to this are the low light periods of dawn and dusk when gamefish are actively feeding. I also run a lot of family charters that include novice anglers and children. Live bait is the ticket to bent rods and smiling faces. In these instances, live shrimp can replace lures to take advantage of the early bite. At some point the pinfish will become a nuisance, requiring a change to baitfish.

Plug, jigs, and spoons are three very effective and versatile lures. High tides first thing in the morning will find my clients casting Rapala X-Raps in the (08) size over bars and edges of grass flats. Snook will also attack them when cast around mangrove shorelines at first light. These baits dive several feet below the surface and are deadly when retrieved back in using sharp twitches with a pause in between. Topwater plugs will elicit explosive strikes! They will generally catch less fish, although often times larger ones. Some of the largest trout will be landed using plugs in shallow water at dawn. Suspending plugs such as the MirrOlure are great for trout over the grass flats.

The lead head jig/plastic tail combination is a proven bait all along the Gulf Coast of Florida. Bass Assassin jigs are very popular in our area. They are available in a wide variety of sizes and colors. My personal favorite is the 3" shad tail on a ¼ ounce jig head. This is a great bait to use when fishing over deeper grass flats for trout, pompano, and whatever else finds it attractive. Light colors such as gold, silver, and pearl work well in clear water while rootbeer and olive are effective in darker water. Lighter jig heads can be used when fishing in shallow water.

Spoons have been around forever, and to this day are still productive lures. They are great for prospecting as they are easy to cast long distances, allowing anglers to cover a lot of water. Spoons basically come in two styles; either weedles with a single hook or with a treble hook. Gold and silver are the two most popular finishes. Weedless spoons are great for enticing redfish in very shallow water. The treble hook version is a good choice when fishing open water. Spanish mackerel are particularly vulnerable to a quickly retrieved silver spoon.

Weather and tide will play a part in my strategy for the morning. Strong tides and a little breeze will usually result in lures being productive later into the morning. Conversely, a still morning with very little water movement will mandate a switch to live bait earlier than normal. Fortunately, bait is usually pretty easy to acquire this time of year. Bird activity will give away the location of the baitfish. Shallow flats near passes are prime spots to find scaled sardines (pilchards) and threadfins. Once located, a good toss or two with a cast net should result in a well full of frisky bait. If bait fish are not visible on the surface, they can be chummed into range using canned mackerel or cat food.

Once the bait is obtained, fishing begins. The technique is pretty simple but as with any other method, subtle nuances can make a big difference. Basically, I anchor up-current of a grass flat in four to eight feet of water. Then, I toss out a handful of bait and if fish are around it won't take long before they start "busting" the baits on the surface. Baits are pinned to a 1/0 hook and cast out; a hookup should promptly ensue. Speckled trout, Spanish mackerel, bluefish, sharks, mangrove snapper, jack crevelle, flounder, and ladyfish are all commonly caught using this technique over the deep grass. It does require a decent cast net, a large live well, and a little patience, but the payoff can be non-stop action all morning long.

Finishing up the charter trying for a snook, redfish, or big jack is also an option with a well full of bait. Anchoring near a mangrove point and chumming will lure the fish into range. I have also landed some large mangrove snapper along with the snook and reds when using this technique. This is a great option as it produces even at mid-day.

September Snappers

There is a relatively untapped fishery in Sarasota in the late summer and early fall. Each year at that time of year schools of mangrove snapper migrate out of the creeks, canals, and backwaters and towards the Gulf of Mexico. Fish will move out into the channels and then the passes. Any structure such as docks, bridges, rip-rap, and oyster bars may hold a bunch of snappers. The abundant structure and deep water make the north end of Siesta Key a great spot for snapper and other gamefish as well. Late in the run (mid-September) ledges and reefs close to shore will hold large numbers of these tasty saltwater panfish.

The key to successful fishing is staying on top of the local migrations. These guys are hungry and will eat, the key is finding them. As a full time guide I have the advantage in that I am out there almost every day and can stay current with prevailing conditions. Generally, I start targeting them in late July. The channel edges of the Intracoastal Waterway from Stickney Pt. Bridge north to Siesta Drive Bridge hold schools of snapper in the late summer. Once the fish are located it is just a matter of staying on them as they migrate out to the Gulf of Mexico. Outgoing tides are best, but not necessary. Another advantage to targeting mangrove snapper is that they will bite later in the morning when the shallow water fishing slows down. Often times, I will hit the grass flats at first light then finish up the morning fishing deeper for the snapper.

One enjoyable aspect of this technique is the simplicity. Basically, I tie on a piece of 20 pound leader and a #1 hook and add a bit of weight, if needed. I prefer a sturdy short shank bait hook. In water ten feet or less a split shot a foot or so from the hook will be all the weight that is needed. This also allows the bait to sink slowly and naturally. When fishing deeper water or in a strong current, more weight will be required. I use a "Knocker rig" in this application. This is simply a sliding egg sinker, usually a quarter or half ounce, threaded on to the leader in front of the hook. The weight actually sits right on top of the eye of the hook. The sliding weight allows a fish to pick up the bait without feeling any resistance.

The most technical aspect of snapper fishing is boat positioning. The best approach is to anchor a cast away up-current of the structure or ledge. The bait can then be presented in a natural manner as it drifts back to the fish. The same theory applies to anglers fishing from docks or the shoreline. Cast structure that is down-current from your position and allow the bait to fall back towards the pilings or rocks. In deep water, such as ledges in the inshore Gulf or the rocks at the mouth of Big Pass, a vertical presentation is best.

While I have fooled plenty of snapper using plugs and jigs, this is primarily a natural bait situation. My personal favorite is a live 2"-3" pilchard. These are not available at bait shops and must be caught with a cast net. While live shrimp work great and are easily obtained, pilchards and small pinfish will catch larger snapper than live shrimp. When using shrimp, anglers will have to sort through smaller fish, but plenty of decent sized fish will also be taken. Baitfish can be hooked through the mouth, nose, throat, or back and shrimp are usually hooked under the horn, right behind the eyes. Cut fresh and frozen bait can also be used successfully. Frozen squid can be cut into strips while chunks of baitfish work well. If available, fresh cut bait will usually be more productive than frozen bait.

Snapper can be delicate in their take and hooking them requires a slightly different technique. I have found the best method has been to cast out the bait and allow it to settle. Sometimes the fish will just take it and run, and if this happens just reel fast and raise the rod tip. But most of the time it begins with a light "tap". There may be several more "taps" before the fish takes the bait. It is crucial to not move the bait at all during this time. Instead, wait patiently for that steady pull and just reel while raising the tip. Don't jerk or set the hook!

One final bonus to this technique is that it will not only produce a tasty snapper dinner, other fish will invariably be caught. Snook, redfish, trout, flounder, sheepshead, drum, pompano, and more with hit a well presented live bait near structure. One particular trip comes to mind. I was catching the last few minutes of the outgoing tide and free lining live shrimp along a drop-off near the Siesta Drive Bridge. The drag and my anglers reel started to scream and when it was over an eight pound permit was resting in the net!

Sheepshead Tricks

I stood there on the dock with my clients, discussing our options. It was February and a blustery winter wind was blowing out of the northwest.

"Let's give it a try", I suggested. "If we are cold and miserable, we will just come back in".

I grabbed a bunch of live shrimp and idled north towards Phillippi Creek. This area has a lot of structure including oyster bars and docks, along with some deeper water. It is also protected from the wind. We anchored up-current of a bar with a drop off into 4 feet of water, tossed out a few pieces of cut up shrimp as chum, and cast out a couple of live shrimp on a #1 hook. It wasn't long before the unmistakable "tap" of a sheepshead was felt. My client waited until a solid pull was felt and reeled quickly while raising the rod tip. The feisty sheepshead was soon landed and placed in the cooler. These striped crustacean-eaters make terrific table fare! Over the next several hours we landed over two dozen sheepies to five pounds, and I never even put the boat on plane. Once again, sheepshead saved the day!

In my opinion, sheepshead are an undervalued gamefish. They fight hard, bite in cold and dirty water when other fish shut down, grow fairly large, and taste great. What more could an angler ask for? They offer a viable and much more cost-effective alternative to offshore bottom fishing. By February they are thick around just about any structure on the north end of Siesta Key in Big Pass and the docks along Bird Key. All of the area bridges, particularly the Twin Bridges going over to St. Armands Key, are reliable spots.

One element of sheepshead fishing that I enjoy is the simplicity. It really does not get any easier than this. However, as in all fishing techniques, there are nuances that will increase an angler's chance of success. Twelve to fifteen pound spinning tackle is ideal, the extra little bit of muscle may be required if larger fish are encountered. The terminal rig consists on a two foot piece of thirty pound shock leader, a little bit of weight, and a #1 or #1/0 live bait hook. In shallow water or when little current is present, a split shot is usually all the weight that is required. When fishing deeper water or in heavy current, a "Knocker rig" can be very effective. This consists of an egg sinker that slides on the leader and rests right on the hook eye. This keeps the bait right on the bottom while still allowing a fish to move off a short distance without feeling any resistance.

Live shrimp are the most popular and easily obtained bait. Fiddler crabs, oyster worms, and sand fleas are terrific baits but are not available at local shops and must be caught. CB's does keep frozen sand fleas and shrimp on hand. While many anglers prefer large shrimp for inshore fishing, in this application the smaller ones can be more effective. Sheepshead have a small mouth; a bite-sized shrimp is perfect. Hooking the shrimp just under the horn is generally the most effective presentation, but if a lot of bites are missed, threading the shrimp on the hook shank should limit the number of missed bites.

   Boat positioning can be critical, particularly in a swift current. Anchoring a short cast up-current from the structure is almost always the best approach. The northwest tip of Siesta Key is a terrific sheepshead spot. The water is over twenty feet deep with a lot of fish-holding structure. This spot is best fished on a slack tide using a vertical presentation.

   There is an old saying regarding sheepshead fishing; "set the hook just before the fish strikes". Of course, that is a joke, but the reality is the take can be very subtle. I have found the following technique to be the best for hooking these delicate feeders. Cast the bait out and allow it to settle on the bottom. Reel up all the slack and keep the line barely tight, but do not move the bait at all. Often times it will begin with a light tap or series of taps. It is crucial to keep the bait perfectly still; moving the bait will usually spook the fish. Wait for a steady pull, then reel quickly and raise the rod tip. The hookup ratio will never be perfect and plenty of bait will be lost to these bait-stealers, but a lot of fish will be caught, too!

Mixed Bag

Fish were boiling fifteen feet behind the boat. Each handful of live pilchards increased the feeding frenzy.

"Cast your baits right into the middle of the action", I instructed my anglers. "You should get bit right away."

Kaitlyn and Danielle cast their baits out and sure enough, an instant "double header"! A pair of attractive young ladies stood on the front of my boat with big smiles and bent rods; it's great to be a fishing guide in Sarasota!

Opportunities abound for anglers who fish the west coast of Florida. Redfish can be sight fished in shallow water, tarpon are targeted along the beaches, and snook will ambush prey along mangrove shorelines. But the majority of fish caught on my charters are done so on the deep grass flats in Sarasota Bay. Danielle and Kaitlyn were in town on a visit from Ontario. Like many of my clients, they had very limited angling experience. In fact, Kaitlyn had never caught a fish before and we certainly fixed that! Fishing the deep grass offers those anglers the chance to catch a lot of fish. These same techniques will produce all along the Gulf Coast.

While the largest fish on the flats are typically found in quite shallow water, the deep grass flats will produce more in terms of action and variety. Anglers who just want to bend the rod and perhaps catch a fish or two for dinner can't do better than drifting the deep grass flats. Spanish mackerel, speckled and silver trout, pompano, bluefish, jack crevelle, mangrove snapper, gag grouper, black sea bass, flounder, cobia, ladyfish and even tarpon are all available at one time of year or another. Every once in a while a snook or redfish will be encountered over open flats deeper than four feet. Mottled expanses of grass in depths from four to eight feet will be the most productive.

Wind, tide, and water clarity all play a role in choosing which flats to fish. The best situation is one in which the wind and tide are moving in the same direction. Generally speaking, incoming tides are preferred but as long as the water is moving, fish can be caught. Flats just inside a pass can be the best spots of all as they flood with bait and clean water from the Gulf of Mexico. The exception to this is right after a cold front passes through. Those flats will soon be covered with "dirty" water due to wind churning up the water in the Gulf. On breezy days it is easier to fish flats that are in protected water as opposed to those in open bays.

Many inshore bays have a shallow bar that runs parallel to the shoreline. These bars generally have a sloping bottom with lush grass that drops off into deep water. These are great spots to fish! Speckled trout and pompano might be taken in the four to five foot depths while Spanish mackerel, bluefish, and ladyfish are usually found on the outer edges of the grass. Points usually have good grass flats on both sides and are also excellent spots to try. Areas near passes will have natural deep channels along with man-made dredged channels. Any grass flat that drops off sharply into deep water can hold fish, particularly on a low tide.

Artificial lures are both very productive and a lot of fun to fish. Casting lures out in front of a drifting boat is a great way to cover a lot of water efficiently. Begin the drift on the up-tide or up-wind side of the flat. Fan cast the area while varying the retrieve. Pay attention to details such as depth and water clarity. If a drift produces good action, idle around and make another pass through the same area. If not, move on to another spot. This technique allows anglers to eliminate unproductive water fairly quickly.

Occasionally, I will anchor when using lures. One recent charter comes to mind. It was very windy and Spanish mackerel were isolated on the up-tide side of grassy points with good current flow. The wind and tide made working these points difficult while drifting. I anchored a short distance away and had my clients cover the small flat using Rapala X-Raps. A fast, erratic retrieve triggered some very exciting strikes! We ended up with a dozen nice Spanish for the box along with speckled trout and ladyfish.

The most popular artificial bait on the west coast of Florida is the lead head jig with a soft plastic body. These baits come in a myriad of colors and styles, but they all basically work the same. And they all catch fish. Bass Assassin jigs come in some great colors and sizes and are very cost-effective to fish. My personal favorite is the red/gold shad tail on a ¼ ounce white jig head. Grub tails and jerk baits are also effective. Dark colors such as olive, green, and rootbeer work well in dark water while gold, silver, and white are good choices in clear water. Chartuese is a great all-round choice and hot pink is a good option when the water is dirty. Scented soft plastic baits such as Gulp! and Trigger-X can make a big difference on days when the fish are reluctant to bite.

Plugs are also effective lures when fished over the deep grass. Suspending plugs such as the venerable MirrOlure are deadly on speckled trout. Both topwater and shallow diving plugs will also catch plenty of fish. The Rapala X-Rap slashbait is a great choice for working areas where fish are breaking on the surface. These lures dive a few feet down and have great action. A fast, erratic retrieve is usually very effective. One disadvantage in using plugs is that the multiple treble hooks can damage small trout.

Silver and gold spoons have been around a long time and they still catch fish. Spanish mackerel love a quickly retrieved silver spoon while speckled trout seem to prefer a slowly wobbling gold spoon. In open water spoons with a treble hook such as the Johnson Sprite are utilized; there is really no need for a weedless spoon in this application.

Fly fisherman can use the same tactics to score on the deep flats. Any fish that will hit a jig will take a weighted fly. The most popular pattern by far is the Clouser Deep Minnow. There are a ton of variations on this fly, but basically it is a hook with some dressing and a weighted eye that allows it to sink. The fly is cast out, allowed to settle for several seconds, and retrieved back in short strips. White, green/white, olive/white, and chartreuse/white Clousers tied on a #1 or #2 hook are the most popular flies. A 7or 8 weight rod with an intermediate sink-tip line works best. Many fly anglers make the mistake of using a floating line. Even with a weighted fly, the line will not get down deep enough when fishing in water over six feet.

While artificial lures are productive, live bait is tough to beat. Shrimp and bait fish are the two most popular live baits. Shrimp are purchased locally while bait fish are usually caught, but they are sometimes available at bait shops. Pinfish, grunts, and "whitebait" are the most commonly used live bait fish. "Whitebait" is a generic term for any shiny white fish that schools up in large numbers (pilchards, threadfin herring, etc.). Match the hook size to the size of the bait. A 1/0 live bait hook is a great all-round choice. I usually free line the bait, but sometimes either a split shot or a float will be required, depending on current flow and depth. Use a long shank hook if cut-offs from mackerel and bluefish become a problem.

A well full of 3" pilchards practically guarantees success. These are caught with a cast net over shallow flats or out on the beach. In the summertime flats near the passes will be covered with these bait fish, especially on an incoming tide. If they are seen on the surface "dimpling", it is easy enough to quietly ease into range by drifting or using a trolling motor. Chumming is a great way to get a bunch of baitfish within range of a cast net. A can of jack mackerel (purchased at your local Publix) and a half loaf of wheat bread is a proven mixture. Add just enough salt water to make a thick paste. Anchor in two to four feet of water on the up-tide side of a flat and sparingly toss pea-sized pieces into the water. The bait should show up within a few minutes.

One charter last summer illustrates how exciting this technique can be. I was fishing the last hour of an outgoing tide early in the morning. Several spots produced a couple of ladyfish and snapper. The third spot was a small grass patch that dropped off into ten feet of water with bait fish activity on the surface. An 18" speckled trout was quickly landed and then Anne-Christine's line started moving off to the side. She reeled up the slack while raising the rod tip, expecting another nice trout. Instead, the mystery fish took off on a long, powerful run, getting perilously close to a channel marker. She was able to turn the fish, then started working it patiently back to the boat. I caught a glimpse of the fish before it took off again; it looked like a pompano. Moments later the mystery was solved as an eight pound permit slid into the net!

Summer Flats Fishing

The morning dawned clear with a light southeast wind. Perfect conditions for summertime fishing here on the Suncoast! I picked up the Schlouch family from Pennsylvania at my home base, CB's Saltwater Outfitters on Siesta Key. With Barry and Deb and their children Stayce and Barry safely aboard, I made the short run to South Lido Key to catch bait. Pilchards are abundant and easy to net first thing in the morning. In short order the livewell was full of frisky bait. After another short run, I anchored up on the edge of a shallow grass flat near Big Pass. For the next three hours we experienced non-stop action on speckled trout, Spanish mackerel, jack crevelle, a cobia, bluefish, ladyfish, sail cats, and small sharks.

The west coast of Florida is famous for great fishing. Glamour species such as snook, redfish, and the mighty tarpon get a lot of attention from anglers, and for good reason. However, many of my charters include novice anglers who really just want to bend the rod and catch a bunch of fish. The deep grass flats in Sarasota are a great place to do just that. Along with the above mentioned species, pompano, flounder, small grouper, snapper, and sea bass are also common catches.

I find the flats adjacent to the passes to be the most consistent summertime spots. Bird Key produces a lot of fish on my charters. It is an area that has seen a lot of dredging resulting in flats that drop off sharply into deep water. The combination of depth change, current, and abundant bait attracts and holds game fish. Early morning is usually the best time to fish, especially on a high tide.

Rigging is very basic. Use a spider hitch to double 3' of the running line and use a double uni-knot to attach 24" of 30 lb. leader. If this seems a bit much, simply tie a small black swivel to your running line then tie on the 30 lb. leader to the swivel. Attach a hook or artificial bait onto the end of the leader and you are ready to fish!

Live bait is tough to beat for both action and variety. A live shrimp fished under a popping cork in four to six feet of water over a grassy bottom is a tried and true method to catch a bunch of speckled trout, along with just about every other species in Sarasota Bay. Tie a 1/0 live bait hook onto the leader then attach a "popping cork" on the line three feet above the hook. When drifting in water deeper than six feet, I prefer to just free line a bait out behind the boat. Shrimp are the most popular live bait. They are available at most local bait shops, are easy to keep alive, and everything eats them!

Live bait fish are extremely effective in the summertime. Pinfish, grunts, and whitebait, (pilchards and threadfins) are the predominant baitfish in our area. A cast net is required for the whitebait. Cast over visible schools of bait or anchor and use chum consisting of jack mackerel and wheat bread to lure the bait within range. Pinfish and grunts can be caught with either a hook and line or a cast net. Catching and keeping baitfish alive is more time consuming, but can pay off big time. One very popular technique is "live bait chumming". This requires a LOT of whitebait, but practically guarantees success. Simply anchor up tide of a likely flat and toss out handfuls of bait at five minute intervals. I usually squeeze the bait before throwing them in, this causes the bait to swim erratically on the surface. Game fish will be drawn in and the action will be non-stop!

A jig/grub combo is by far the most popular artificial lure on the west coast of Florida. A ¼ ounce jig head with a plastic grub is a deadly bait when fished over the grass flats. I prefer gold in clear water and rootbeer or olive in darker water. Don't let the myriad of colors and styles confuse you, they all either imitate shrimp or baitfish and are for the most part fished in the same manner. Cast the jig out, allow a few seconds for it to sink and twitch the rod tip sharply. Let the lure fall on a tight line, most strikes occur as the bait is falling; the helpless look triggers the bite. Keeping the rod tip at ten o'clock and allowing the jig to fall on a tight line will allow anglers to feel more bites. Grubs with a shad tail or curly tail that mimic baitfish can be worked with a steady retrieve. Scented soft plastics such as Trigger-X and Gulp! baits are more expensive but can make a difference on days when the fish are a little fussy.

Plugs are another great choice for anglers who prefer to cast artificial lures. Rapala X-Raps in the (08) size are my personal favorite. They cast well and have great action. Cast the lure our and retrieve it back to the boat with sharp twitches followed by a short pause. As in all lure fishing, vary the retrieve until one is found that produces strikes.

Set the alarm, get out there early, and experience some action that is as hot as the weather!

Fly Fishing Made Easy

Candice was distracted by several bottlenose dolphin that were playing a hundred feet off to the right.

"You need to start stripping or your line is going to hang up in the grass", I instructed her.

She gave me a sheepish grin and began to retrieve the fly back in. On the fifth strip the line got tight and shot off to the side. The fish did not leap as of the water as the several previous ladyfish had, making me wonder if perhaps she had hooked a different species. My hunch was confirmed as several moments later a two pound pompano came to the net; an unexpected but most welcome surprise! Ironically, the dolphins were responsible for the catch; their distraction enabled the fly to sink all the way down to the bottom where they typically feed.

Candice is an East Sarasota country girl who loves horses, mudding, shooting guns, but most of all fishing. Although fairly experienced with spin fishing, she was intrigued by the idea of fly fishing yet had no idea where to start. After an hour of casting practice and another hour of fishing, she hooked and landed a half-dozen ladyfish and that nice pompano! This article is aimed towards other anglers that are interested in trying fly fishing but are overwhelmed by the prospect.

The primary difference between spin fishing and fly fishing is that in spin fishing the lure or bait provides the weight and the line is the connection between the hook and the reel. In the fly fishing the line is cast as the fly weighs next to nothing. Keeping that in mind, the tackle is similar but with some significant differences.

Matching fly tackle is very easy as rods, reels and lines are designated by "weight". That number appears on rods and lines as the abbreviation "Wt". It is always best to match the line, rod, and reel with the same weight line. For most inshore saltwater applications, an 8 weight (8wt) outfit is ideal. Fly rods also come in different actions; a "mid-flex" is the most forgiving and is the best choice for a novice angler.

The reel in fly fishing is not used all that much; it basically just stores the line, unless a larger fish is hooked and the fish starts taking drag. The fly line is manipulated by hand for the most part. The best choice would be a large arbor saltwater reel with a good drag system. Fly reels are "single action", which means that there is no gear multiplication as with a spinning reel. Also, the reel will spin backwards when a fish runs, so keep your knuckles clear!

Fly lines are an extremely important part of the system and a quality line is well worth the cost. Lines come in weights as rods and reels do, but there are also a variety of types of lines. Basically, they are either floating, intermediate sink tip, or full sinking. Intermediate sink tip lines are the most versatile for fishing the relatively shallow depths on inshore Florida waters. One mistake that visiting freshwater fly anglers make is trying to use full floating lines. They are easier to cast but will not allow the fly to sink down far enough into the water column. Two hundred yards of 20 lb. test "backing" is spooled up behind the fly line.

Fly selection can also be overwhelming and confusing to a beginning fly angler. Much like spin fishing, there are a myriad of choices in color, size, and style. Most flies mimic either a baitfish or crustacean. One of the most popular and effective fly patterns is the Clouser Deep Minnow. It consists of a hook, small weighted lead eyes, and some bucktail or synthetic dressing. Sound familiar? It should, it is basically a bucktail jig, a lure that has proven itself over time. It is a good idea to have unweighted flies as well, and Lefty's Deceiver is a great choice. White is a good color to start with but using a fly that matches the colors that are locally productive should produce.

A leader is used between the end of the fly line and the fly. In freshwater fishing the leader is very important, tapering down which allows the small fly to "turn over" and land softly. Tapered leaders really are not required in saltwater fly fishing. Most saltwater flies have a little weight and will extend the leader out. In most cases, a 6 piece of 30 lb. fluorocarbon will be sufficient.

In summary, heading to a local fly shop and purchasing an 8wt rod in a mid-flax action, matching reel spooled with 200 yards of backing, intermediate sink-tip line, a spool of 30 lb. fluorocarbon leader, and a small selection of Clouser Minnows and Deceivers (the shop can help with locally productive patterns) will prepare a novice fly angler with the equipment needed to get started.

Once the proper equipment is acquired it is time to go fishing. Well, not quite! Before heading out to the water some casting practice will be required. It is best to become a bit comfortable and proficient in casting and managing the line BEFORE heading out to fish. There are many good resources out there but one of the best options is to take a class given by a local shop, guide, or outfitter.

Now that the tackle is in hand and the angler has the ability to cast forty feet, it is time to go fishing! As previously mentioned, the fly is manipulated by hand rather than with the rod and reel. The fly is cast out, allowed to sink to the desired depth and then retrieved back using short "strips" with the rod tip low and pointed at the fly. When a fish takes the fly, the line is pulled taut with the stripping hand and once tension is felt, the rod tip is raised up high. This is called a "strip set". Resisting the urge to set the hook or jerk the tip up will result in more hooked fish. Smaller fish can be brought in using smooth strips, coiling the line below the reel. With larger fish, use the stripping hand to feed line back out while manually applying some tension. Once all of the slack line is taken up, the fish is "on the reel" and can be fought using the rod and reel. If no bite occurs, the line is picked up and cast out again.

The best approach when starting off is to target species that will provide action and variety, it is better to "practice" on the less challenging species. This will give the novice angler both experience and confidence. The good news is that local knowledge that is already possessed will produce for fly anglers. Any fish that will hit an artificial lure can be taken on fly. Here in Sarasota that means drifting the deeper grass flats in search of speckled trout, Spanish mackerel, bluefish, ladyfish, and other species. As with spin fishing, casting in front of a drifting boat can be very productive. It will take some time to learn to manage the line while casting, fishing, and catching, especially when it is a bit breezy. Anglers will also be successful wading and fishing from shore.

Thinking about giving the long rod a try? If so, give it a chance, but be prepared to be "hooked" for life!

Fall Beach Fishing

Contrary to popular belief, autumn does arrive in Florida, although the changes can be fairly subtle. While still fairly warm, evening temperatures are a tad lower and the days are a little shorter. Fish are very much in tune with these changes and it affects their behavior. In Sarasota where I fish, on the west coast, the arrival of Spanish mackerel and false albacore just off the beaches in the inshore Gulf of Mexico officially signals the fall fishing season. This is great sport and it does not require a large boat or fancy gear to take advantage of this bonanza.

The reason for this fantastic fishing is simple; bait, and LOTS of it! As the water and land temperatures drop, the weather pattern changes. The sea breezes will be gone and high pressure systems will bring northeast winds both during the day and in the evening. The result will be clear, calm water along the beaches, attracting huge schools of baitfish which in turn attracts the gamefish. Saltwater fishing can be pretty basic, "Find the groceries; find the fish". Other species will also be encountered when fishing "Out on the beach". Jack crevelle, bluefish, ladyfish, king mackerel, cobia, sharks, and even tarpon will follow the forage to take advantage of the abundance of forage.

As a full-time fishing guide I rely on live bait a majority of the time to provide action for my clients. In this application, artificial lures are not only extremely productive but are a lot of fun to fish! Quite often schools of "breaking" fish will be seen terrorizing the helpless baitfish on the surface. Opportunistic gulls and terns will be picking at the scraps as well. This is a sight that will stir any angler's soul and is the perfect situation to use an artificial lure. The strikes will be immediate and savage! Of course, a frisky live baitfish or shrimp will very seldom go unmolested.

My "go to" lure for fishing the inshore Gulf is #8 Rapala X-Rap slashbait. It perfectly mimics the small pilchards, glass minnows, and threadfin herring that the gamefish are feeding on. Olive is my favorite color with white being a close second. The lure is simply cast out into the bait and retrieved back with sharp twitches and a pause in between. X-Raps can also be trolled along when there is not any surface activity; they are a great "locator" bait. The venerable jig and grub combo also works well, with the 4" Bass Assassin Sea Shad being my personal favorite. Silver spoons will also produce plenty of fish. The same tackle that is used for speckled trout and redfish will work fine in this application. My preferred rig is a 10 lb. spinning outfit with monofilament line, the last 5' doubled with a Spider Hitch, then 30" of 30 lb. fluorocarbon leader is added using a double Uni-knot, then the lure or hook completes the rig.

Fly anglers can certainly take advantage of this situation as well. An 8wt outfit with a weight forward floating line is a good choice. The leader should be 8' of 30 lb. fluorocarbon and any small white fly will produce well, with D.T. Special and Clouser Minnow patterns being the most popular.

Once rigged up and ready, it is time to go fishing! Often times the fish will be schooled up just outside the passes, particularly on an outgoing tide. Any bird or surface activity should be investigated. Sometimes just a couple of terns diving will clue an angler into the location of a school. If nothing is happening at the pass, simply cruise down the beach on plane but at as slow a speed as possible in order to completely scan the area. Once a school of actively feeding fish is located, determine whether they are mackerel or albies. Spanish will generally stay up in the same spot for a longer period of time. False albacore can be much more difficult to get on; they move fast and change directions constantly. But, there is no greater sport than catching a big albie on light tackle or fly!

In either case, patience will pay off! Charging into the school on plane will usually shut down the bite. Instead, cut the motor up-wind of the fish and drift down on them until in casting range or use the electric trolling motor if so equipped. Trolling the edges will also work well but avoid driving through the middle of the school. Sarasota County has an extensive artificial reef program with 3 nice reefs within 2 miles of shore just off Lido Key. These are a great back-up plan (as is any reef or hard bottom area) in the event that surface activity is absent as they almost always hold bait and fish.

Later in the morning as the sun comes up, particularly if the water is clear, anglers will do well to look for bait balls. These appear as large dark spots in the water. NEVER pass up a nice, big ball of bait as there will usually be predator fish on the edges. Anglers seeking larger game will score consistently on sharks by putting out a chunk of mackerel under a cork on a larger rig with a steel leader. Free-lining a large live threadfin herring at the edges will also produce some larger fish. Do not be surprised if a cobia, king mackerel, or even a tarpon are hooked as well!

Shore bound anglers can get in on the action as well. While false albacore seldom venture in close enough to be caught from land, Spanish mackerel, jacks, bluefish, ladyfish, and more will often cruise within casting range while feasting upon the abundance of forage. The same lures, baits, flies, and techniques that produce for anglers in boats will also allow surf casters to achieve success.

Monthly Fishing Forecasts

January

January fishing in Sarasota is all about the weather, pure and simple. Angling success is determined by the ability to adapt to the existing weather conditions. Tides will often times be very low in the morning. Couple that with a northeast wind, and the flats will not have very much water on them. Water temperatures will be at their annual low. It is time to change tactics!

I spend a lot of my time fishing the area around Siesta Key in the winter. Both passes and the surrounding flats will be productive under ideal conditions. Weekly fronts will stir up the Gulf, bringing cold, dirty water in through the passes and up onto the nearby flats. However, the area down south stays protected, and this will result in better fishing. Extreme low tides will force the fish off of the flats and into the channel. This actually makes locating them easier. 1/4 ounce Bass Assassin jigs in olive and rootbeer/gold are very productive, as is a shrimp free lined with a small split shot. Speckled trout, ladyfish, jack crevelle, and pompano will be the primary catches, but sheepshead, grouper, flounder, and bluefish will also be found in the deep water.

As the tide rises and the day warms up, fish will move out of the deep channel and up onto the flats to feed. A late Afternoon high tide can offer great fishing for speckled trout, with jigs and live shrimp under a popping cork are producing the best bites. The flats south of Spanish Point are very productive, but any flat in four to six feet of water with grass will hold fish, keep moving until you find them.

Creeks and residential canals are great spots to fish this month. Besides offering protection from harsh winds, they provide cover for bait, which attracts fish, and the water is normally a few degrees warmer. A large hand-picked shrimp is a great bait for redfish, snook, sheepshead, drum, and jacks. Deeper water is the key, find a dock or area in a creek with a little more depth and there should be fish there. A few pieces of shrimp tossed out as chum can help get the bite going. Rapala X-Raps are a terrific artificial bait to use in creeks. They are deadly on snook and jacks, and a lot of water can be covered quickly. Go with smaller lures this time of year to imitate the bait that is present.

Oyster bars are abundant in this area and are fish magnets. Small crabs and worms will hide in the crevices, and this attracts game fish, especially redfish and sheepshead. A 1/8 ounce jig tipped with a tiny piece of shrimp is a deadly bait to use when fishing the bars. Scented soft plastics like Trigger –X and Gulp baits also work very well. I like darker, natural colors such as olive, rootbeer, and smoke. Fish them as slowly as possible without snagging on the bottom. Of course, a live shrimp will also catch plenty of fish. A float may be required to keep the shrimp from hanging up in the oysters.

Sheepshead will be around in good numbers by the end of the month. Unlike most species, these tasty saltwater panfish do not mind the dirty water. Structure in the passes, bridges, docks, and oyster bars throughout the area may hold sheepies. Shrimp are an effective bait and are easily obtained. Live shrimp are best, but frozen shrimp will catch fish, too. Use a #1 live bait hook on 24" of 30 lb leader and enough weight to hold the bottom.

February

February is the last month of winter here in Sarasota. There will be days when it feels like spring is in the air. But, weather patterns will still be unstable, and fishing will follow suit. Being flexible and understanding how weather affects fish behavior will be the key to angling success this month. On many mornings the tide will be very low, especially with a hard northeast wind following a cold front. Under these conditions, fishing the afternoon high tide is often a better choice. Also avoid the areas near the passes after a blow, the cold and dirty water is not conducive to success.

One species that anglers can count on most every trip in February is sheepshead. They bite better in cold, dirty water than most other species do. Also, redfish, black drum, and flounder will be caught on the same structure and using the same techniques that are effective for sheepies. Basically, any structure will attract sheepshead. From the rocks at the west end to the Siesta Drive Bridge on the east side, the north end of Siesta Key is a great area to fish. Deep water, docks, rocks, seawalls, and rip-rap will attract and hold fish. All of the bridges and docks in both Big Pass and New Pass may hold fish, as well as the docks and oyster bars south to Albee Rd.

The preferred rig is a #1 live bait hook with a 24" piece of 20 lb leader and just enough weight to hold bottom. Live and frozen shrimp, fiddler crabs, sand fleas, and oyster worms are the top baits. Shrimp are the easiest bait to obtain and work great. Sheepshead bite very lightly. Usually, it starts with several light "taps". It is important not to move the bait at all, the fish will sense that something is wrong. Instead, wait for a steady pull, then reel fast and raise the rod tip sharply.

Casting jigs while drifting with the tide in the passes will be productive when the water is clear. A ¼ oz. Bass Assassin jig head with a gold grub tail is a very effective bait. Pompano, bluefish, ladyfish, and maybe an early-arriving Spanish mackerel will be the primary catches. Try the shallow bars and the deeper channels, keep moving until the fish are located, then concentrate drifts on that area.

The deeper grass flats all throughout the area will be productive for speckled trout this month. Incoming tides a couple hours before high tide are usually the best times to fish. Again, avoid the areas around the passes when dirty water is present. The area further south, from Stickney Pt. to Marker #19 in Nokomis, stays protected, resulting in reliable February fishing. Bass Assassin jigs, Rapala suspending plugs, gold spoons, and live shrimp under a popping cork are all effective baits. Pompano, jack crevelle, ladyfish, and bluefish all feed over the deep grass.

Snook will be found in creeks and residential canals, along with redfish, drum, flounder, sheepshead, and jacks. Rapala X-Raps, scented soft plastics, and live shrimp will all produce fished near structure in creeks and canals. A slow presentation will be more productive in the cooler water.

Extreme low tides offer opportunities for anglers who enjoy sight fishing for redfish. The area on the east side, north of Long Bar is very shallow with many small potholes, resulting in idea conditions to find tailing reds. The flats off of the Ringling Mansion and Buttonwood Harbor are also good spots to fish. Scented soft plastic baits, weedless gold spoons, and live shrimp are the preferred baits.

March

March is a great month to fish on Siesta Key. It is the first month of spring, both on the calendar and outside. The list of available species is long; snook, redfish, trout, pompano, cobia, king and Spanish mackerel, sheepshead, flounder, snapper, grouper, jack crevelle, and sharks just to name a few.

Big Pass will be very productive this month, particularly when the water is clean. Ladyfish are usually thick, with bluefish, mackerel, and pompano mixed in. The sheepshead run will peak this month. Just about any structure near either pass will hold these tasty critters. A live shrimp fished on the bottom should result in a fish dinner pretty easily.

Speckled trout will be schooled up over deep grass flats throughout the entire area. Incoming tides are best, but as long as the water is moving the fish will bite. A live shrimp under a noisy cork is a proven trout slayer. Bass Assassin Sea Shad baits on a ¼ ounce jig head will fool many fish, too. Pompano, mackerel, ladyfish, bluefish, jacks, and a stray cobia will also be encountered when fishing over the grass flats. These are large areas, the key to success is to keep moving until fish are located, do not spend too much time in one spot if it is not producing.

Snook will move out of their winter retreats on their way out to the Gulf to spawn. The Myakka River will still produce some good fish as they migrate down river. Any structure with a depth change is a likely place to catch a snook. Docks, bridges, and oyster bars are all very productive, especially those with some current. Plugs and scented soft plastic baits are the top choices, along with a large hand-picked shrimp.

Surf fishing should be good for a variety of species providing the water is clear and not roiled up. Whiting, silver trout, flounder, pompano, Spanish mackerel, and ladyfish with hit both live shrimp and artificial lures. A jig tipped with a small piece of shrimp works well bounced along the bottom. Mackerel and ladyfish will hit flash lures such as silver spoons and plugs. I live shrimp fished on the bottom with just enough weight to get down is a simple but effective technique and will catch anything that swims. Anglers targeting pompano will do well with live or frozen sand fleas.

The beach should come alive this month, provided the winds cooperate. Spanish and king mackerel will invade the area, along with cobia, sharks, and false albacore. The inshore reefs off of Lido Key are a great place to start, they hold a lot of fish. Trolling spoons and plugs is a deadly technique and will fill the cooler in short order. For more sport, look for breaking fish on the surface and cast plugs, spoons, or flies out into the frenzy, a vicious strike should occur immediately!

April

Mother Nature is usually kind to us this month. Warming temperatures signal fish migrations both in Sarasota Bay and the Gulf of Mexico. April should offer incredible fishing for a variety of species.

Big Pass and New Pass will be alive with fish migrating in and out of the bay this month. Spanish mackerel, bluefish, pompano, and ladyfish should be plentiful. Pompano prefer a small white or chartreuse jig bounced along the bottom while the mackerel are often found higher in the water column or breaking on the surface. There is nothing more exciting than casting a surface plug on light tackle or a fly into a feeding frenzy!

Action on the deep flats will be very good for speckled trout, pompano, Spanish mackerel, bluefish, and ladyfish. The best flats to fish will be from Siesta Drive north to Long Bar. Flats that are near both passes will be especially productive. A ¼ ounce Bass Assassin Sea Shad is a great lure to prospect with; a lot of water can be covered and just about every species will hit it. Plugs work very well when surface activity is seen, they also are a great lure to troll slowly and locate schools of fish. Silver and gold spoons are another good choice. Live bait is always a great choice, too. A live shrimp free lined or fished under a noisy float is a deadly technique.

The area between Siesta Drive and Blackburn Point will be good for snook as they migrate out towards the beach to spawn. Any point, oyster bar, dock, or creek mouth that drops off into deeper water is a likely spot to try. High, outgoing tides are best. Plugs cover a lot of water and result in vicious strikes while jigs require more patience but will fool more redfish along with snook. Don't be surprised when a big jack crevelle or trout inhales an offering meant for a snook or red.

This has been a good season for sheepshead and while it is past its peak there should still be plenty of these tasty saltwater panfish around. Docks, seawalls, and bridges near passes will hold sheepies. A live shrimp fished on the bottom will fool them, along with snapper, grouper, and flounder.

Surf fishing should be very good for Spanish mackerel, ladyfish, flounder, pompano, and more. Live or frozen shrimp fished near the bottom with a little weight works well. Spoons, plugs, and jigs will also catch plenty of fish, too.

April is a great month for anglers with a small boat and not a lot of experience to catch big fish. The beaches and inshore artificial reefs will be thick with king and Spanish mackerel, along with false albacore and the occasional cobia. Trolling spoons is very easy and deadly on all species. Sight casting to schools of breaking fish is fantastic sport using spinning or fly tackle.

May

May is a transition month in Sarasota. Although the calendar says it is still spring, by late May it will definitely feel like summer time. Pelagic species such as king and Spanish mackerel will have migrated north, inshore fishing will be best early and late, and giant tarpon will invade the inshore Gulf of Mexico, a sure sign that summer is here!

Speckled trout fishing should be outstanding in May. It has been unseasonably warm and bait will be scattered all throughout the bay. The flats near Big Pass will be productive. Casting Bass Assassin 4" Sea Shad baits on ¼ ounce jig heads in front of a drifting boat will produce a lot of speckled trout. A live shrimp under a noisy cork is a deadly technique for catching trout. Pinfish, grunts, and pilchards will produce less fish, but generally larger ones.

The shallow flats will be very active as they flood with bait. A low, incoming tide is the best time to search for reds and snook in the skinny water. Fish will stage in holes and deeper water then move up onto the shallow flats as the tide floods. Scented soft plastics, weedless gold spoons, topwater plugs, and live bait are all effective. Lures work best when looking for fish, water can be covered quickly. Live bait is best once the fish are located. Some of the largest trout will also be found in shallow water.

Snook will be moving out to the beaches and will be scattered out all over. Mangrove points and bars near the passes should hold snook, as will structure in both Big Pass and New Pass. Outgoing tides are preferred, but as long as the water is moving, fish can be caught. Plugs are great baits that cover a lot of water quickly and are great fun to fish. Jigs and other soft plastics work well, too. Anglers who are proficient with a cast net will load up the well with pilchards and catch a lot of fish.

Surf fishing should be excellent and by the end of May there will be decent numbers of snook in the surf line. Small white jigs and flies work well on snook, as does live bait fish. Silver spoons cast out and retrieved in quickly will fool mackerel and ladyfish. Live shrimp will fool a variety of species.

By the middle of the month, many guides and recreational anglers will be focusing on one of the most exciting angling challenges found anywhere, light tackle casting to giant tarpon! This is truly world class big game fishing. Tarpon that migrate up our coasts are large fish that average 80 pounds, but reach over 200 pounds. 25-30 lb spinning tackle and 12 weight fly rods are used most often. A live crab is the preferred bait, but live pinfish and other bait fish work well, too. These baits are fairly light and spinning tackle works best to cast and present baits

June

June will find Sarasota beaches lined with anglers in search of the ultimate gamefish, tarpon, especially early in the month. Catching these giants is really not complicated. Rig a 25 lb. spinning outfit with 36" of 80lb flourocarbon leader and a 5/0 hook, then position the boat 100 yards off the beach and cast a live crab, pinfish, sardine, lure, or fly at any pod that presents itself.

One benefit of the popularity of tarpon fishing is that pressure in the bay will be light. With many anglers "out on the beach" the bays are relatively un-pressured. Bait will be plentiful, those proficient in cast-netting will have no problem filling their live-wells with frisky pilchards. Once the well is filled, you can choose to anchor up on a likely spot or drift across a large flat. Live shrimp is also deadly on most species, but as we move into summer the pinfish become more of a problem. Anglers casting artificial baits will do well with jigs, Rapala X-Raps, and spoons.

The flats around both passes will be productive for speckled trout, Spanish mackerel, pompano, bluefish, and ladyfish. Shrimp under a popping cork, live pilchards, and artificial lures are all productive baits. 4" Bass Assassin Sea Shad baits in Red/Gold Shiner and Glow/Chartreuse on a ¼ oz. jig head will account for plenty of fish.

Redfish will begin to school up on the shallow flats this month. A low, incoming tide is preferred, the fish will move up onto the flats with the rising tide. Scented soft plastics, weedless spoons, and topwater plugs work well for those who prefer to cast artificial lures. Live bait can be extremely effective, anchoring up and fishing potholes is a proven technique.

You can count on one thing in June in Sarasota; it is going to be hot! One way to beat the heat is to fish in the evening and at night. Snook are nocturnal by nature and feed heavily in the dark. Working lighted docks and bridges is the most popular night fishing method. Anchor a cast away up-current of the light, then toss a live or artificial shrimp, baitfish, small jig, plug, or fly into the shadow line of the light. You may also catch mangrove snapper, speckled trout, ladyfish, jacks, and maybe even a tarpon fishing the bridges at night.

Beach fishing for snook was decent last season, and it should be good again this summer, especially with the mild winter that we had. Walk the beach in the morning, looking for snook in the surf line. Cast out a small spoon, plug, or jig in front of any snook that you spot. This is a great time to break out the fly rod, white baitfish patterns are best. Flounder, trout, ladyfish, mackerel, jacks, pompano, and other species will hit live and frozen shrimp and jigs off the Siesta Key beaches in June.

July

July fishing can be excellent, but tactics need to be a little different and windows of opportunity are smaller. It is simply too hot to fish in the middle of the day. Early morning will be the most reliable time to fish, evenings are good too, but frequent thunderstorms can make planning a trip difficult. Anglers who don't mind fishing in the dark will have success at night, and they will beat the summer heat!

Action on the deep grass flats from the north end of Siesta Key should be very good for speckled trout, along with bluefish, Spanish mackerel, ladyfish, pompano, and jacks. A high tide in the morning is favored for anglers to drift the flats and cast Bass Assassin jigs, Rapala plugs, spoons, and live shrimp under a popping cork. Netting up a bunch of shiners and chumming the deep flats will usually result in non-stop action.

The flats and oyster bars south of CB's Saltwater Outfitters at Stickney Pt. down to Blackburn Pt. will hold some nice trout in July, and that area gets very little pressure in the summertime. The key is water temperature; if it is too high the bait and gamefish will not be there. Redfish and snook will also cruise the bars and shorelines in search of prey. Areas that drop off quickly into three or four feet will be the most productive spots. A hand-picked shrimp is deadly fished early in the morning on a high tide. Anglers choosing artificial lures will score with topwater and shallow diving plugs, scented soft plastics, and weedless gold spoons.

Redfish will begin to school up in July and can be caught in very shallow water The largest trout also prefer shallow water, so don't be surprised if a "gator" intercepts an offering meant for a redfish. These fish should be released unharmed, they are the female breed stock and are crucial to a healthy trout fishery.

Night fishing will be exciting and productive in July. Lighted docks and bridges attract glass minnows and shrimp, which in turn attract the gamefish. Snook are abundant, but trout, reds, jacks, ladyfish, and snapper will also be caught at night. Live shrimp works very well free lined in the current with little or no weight. A 24" piece of 25 lb flourocarbon leader and a 1/0 live bait hook is the basic rig. Lures will also catch fish, but can be difficult to cast at night. Fly fisherman will score with a small white snook fly such as the Grassett's Snook Minnow tied on a #4 hook.

Tarpon will still be plentiful in the Gulf of Mexico, although the anglers will not be. The large schools will have broken up, and although the fish don't show as well, they eat better. Pinfish and crabs drifted out 6 feet under a cork at first light will catch tarpon in July. Point of Rocks on Siesta Key is a proven spot to fish.

August

There is a little secret here on Siesta Key; the fishing is terrific in August! Many anglers assume that the heat slows down the action, but this is far from true. The reality is that due to daily rain showers, the water temperature is actually lower in August than it is in June. Hordes of bait fish cover the flats. This combination results in excellent conditions for anglers to succeed. The best action will be early morning, late afternoon, and at night.

Snook love the infusion of fresh water into the bay. Snook migrate back into the bays after spawning out on the beach in August. Shallow diving plugs such as the Rapala X-Rap are very effective baits. They cover a lot of water and produce explosive strikes. Scented soft plastics also work well. Live shrimp, pinfish, and pilchards will also catch a lot of snook, particularly once the fish are located. Outgoing tides at first light and in the evening are the best times to fish.

Redfish will begin to school up in large numbers in August. The bars south of Siesta Drive are worth a try. Weedless gold spoons and scented soft plastic baits on a 1/8 ounce jig head are proven baits. Hand-picked shrimp cast into pot holes is a deadly technique, too. Low, incoming tides are best.

The deep grass flats on the north end of Siesta Key will be good spots to target speckled trout. High tides in the morning will produce plenty of fish. Spanish mackerel, pompano, bluefish, ladyfish, jack crevelle, sharks, small gag grouper, and mangrove snapper will also be caught by anglers drifting the deep grass. A live shrimp under a popping cork works very well. A jig with a grub tail is the preferred artificial bait but plugs and spoons are also effective.

The bars Stickney Pt. south to Blackburn Pt. will hold some very nice trout along with a few redfish. This area does not get a lot of pressure in the summertime. This is an early morning bite and a high tide is preferred.

In the last several years mangrove snapper fishing has been outstanding! Grass flats that drop off into deep water with some current flow should produce plenty of nice snapper this month. Live bait works best and baitfish will usually catch larger fish than shrimp. A 1/0 live bait hook tied on a 24" piece of 20 pound flourocarbon leader with just enough split shot to get to the bottom is the simple but effective rig.

Surf casters should have opportunities for snook, the beach fishing for snook this year has been outstanding. Small artificial lures such as white jigs and small plugs work well, while live shrimp and baitfish will score more consistently. Other species such as Spanish mackerel, ladyfish, drum, trout, pompano, and flounder will be taken as well. The best conditions are an east wind and incoming tide.

September

September is the month that redfish begin schooling up in Sarasota. The expansive shallow flats in Sarasota Bay are traditionally the most productive areas to fish. A low, incoming tide in the morning is preferred, allowing anglers to see the large schools of reds. As the tide rises, the fish will work up from the edges of flats and holes onto the grass to feed. Locating the fish can be difficult under flood tide conditions; there is just too much water up on the flat to effectively sight fish.

Speckled trout fishing has been outstanding this year and this should continue in September. Deeper flats will produce more fish, while the larger specimens may be found in shallow water. A Rapala Skitter Walk or X-Rap worked over bars at first light is a deadly technique for fooling gator trout. Along with trout, anglers fishing the deep grass will catch a variety of species this month including bluefish, Spanish mackerel, mangrove snapper, pompano, gag grouper, and ladyfish. Both live bait and artificial lures will catch plenty of fish. A Bass Assassin grub on a ¼ ounce jig head is a great choice for anglers who enjoy casting artificial lures. Olive (08) X-Raps and other plugs are also effective along with gold and silver spoons. A live shrimp under a popping cork is a time-proven technique for catching "specks" on the West Coast of Florida.

Snook will migrate from the beaches back into the bays. Both passes will be great spots to fish, especially on afternoon outgoing tides. The bars and mangrove shorelines along Siesta Key are prime spots as the fish move towards their fall feeding areas. Artificial baits will allow anglers to cover more water, while a well full of pilchards practically guarantees success. Redfish, large speckled trout, jack crevelle, and mangrove snapper may also be encountered while pursuing the mighty snook. Lighted docks and bridges are snook magnets and will provide great action for anglers looking to catch fish and escape the summer sun. Live and artificial shrimp free lined in the tide are deadly, as are small white flies.

Surf fishing off the Siesta Key beaches should be good for snook, ladyfish, Spanish mackerel, pompano, and other species. Point of Rocks is the best spot as there is a lot of fish-holding structure, but any stretch of beach is likely to produce. Live bait such as shrimp and small bait fish works great. A #1 live bait hook with a short piece of leader and a split shot is the preferred rig. Spoons, plugs, and jigs are also effective baits in the surf.

The rocks and bridges in Big Pass will be excellent spots to target mangrove snapper this month. These tasty saltwater panfish will be migrating out of the bay and into the Gulf of Mexico. Slack tides are the best times to drop a live shrimp or bait fish along the structure. Don't be surprised if a big snook intercepts a bait meant for a mang!

October

October is a fabulous month to be fishing in Sarasota! Shorter, cooler days result in water temperatures dropping into the low 70s, bait will be thick in the bays and out on the beach, and that will attract the gamefish. Many species are going to be caught using a variety of angling tactics. Redfish will still be schooled up on the flats in the north bay, snook will be in the bays, speckled trout, pompano, and Spanish mackerel will be feeding on the deep grass flats, and the beach should be outstanding for king and Spanish mackerel, false albacore, cobia, sharks, and even a stray tarpon.

Anglers with small boats can catch large fish this month. The techniques and methods are really pretty simple. Mornings that dawn with easterly winds will find the inshore Gulf of Mexico flat and calm. Pods of baitfish will be seen on the surface, along with schools of feeding fish. Threadfins caught on Sabiki rigs and free lined out behind the boat will catch just about everything. Use a 4/0 hook on a 24" piece of 80 lb. leader and drift the bait on the outer edges of the bait pods. If cutoffs from kings or sharks become a problem, use a short piece of wire. Shrimp and smaller baitfish work well on the Spanish mackerel and albies, use a 2/0 long shank hook on 40 ln leader.

There is no greater sport than sight fishing "breaking" fish. Actively working gamefish will hit spoons, Rapala X-Raps, jigs, and flies. Silver and white are good colors to start out with. Often times, small baits will be needed, especially for the false albacore, they can be quite fussy. Patient anglers will score more often than those driving aggressively into the fish. Getting in the area and just sitting patiently while waiting for an opportunity will produce more fish than "running and gunning". If the fish are not showing well or if there is a chop on the surface, trolling Rapalas and Clark spoons on planers can be deadly. The inshore artificial reefs are fish magnets and success is practically guaranteed for trollers in October.

Casting jigs while drifting over deep grass flats will produce a lot of fish in October. Speckled trout, pompano, bluefish, mackerel, jacks, and ladyfish will hit a red/gold Bass Assassin grub on a ¼ ounce jig head. Rootbeer and olive are also productive colors. Spoons, plugs, and flies will also work well, as will live or artificial shrimp under a noisy cork. These same lures fished in Big Pass and New Pass will result in plenty of hook-ups as the fish migrate from the Gulf into Sarasota Bay. Fish right on the bottom for pompano and just under the surface for blues and macks.

Redfish will still be schooled up, but their numbers will be diminishing. The shallow flats in the north bay near Long Bar and Buttonwood Harbor are great spots to try. The docks and oyster bars off of Siesta Key will also produce redfish, along with snook, snapper, flounder, and drum. A live shrimp is a a great bait for fishing docks, scented soft plastics such as Trigger-X baits are very effective working bars and points. A high, outgoing tide is best.

Snook will be back in the bays and feeding aggressively on the flats, bars, and mangrove shorelines. Shallow diving plugs such as an (08) olive X-Rap are very effective and allow anglers to cover water quickly. Creek mouths, points, bars, and docks that have current are likely ambush spots. Bridges will produce a lot of snook for nocturnal anglers.

November

November offers Sarasota anglers diverse opportunities. A wide variety of species are available this month, and multiple techniques will be successful. The key is adapting to the conditions; weather will become a factor at times. Water temperatures will be falling as it cools off and the days become shorter, and this will trigger fish to feed.

Both Big Pass and New Pass will be productive spots to fish this month. Pompano will be targeted by many anglers, along with Spanish mackerel, bluefish, and ladyfish. Drifting with the tide and bouncing a jig off the bottom is a proven technique to catch pompano and other species. Yellow, white, and chartreuse pompano jigs work very well in deep, swift water. These jigs are small and compact, allowing them to sink quickly. These same jigs are effective in shallow water and on bars when cast out and retrieved back to the boat using short hops. Spoons and Rapala plugs are very effective when breaking fish are seen working in the passes.

Pompano will also be taken on the deep grass flats, as will speckled trout, bluefish, mackerel, jack crevelle and other species. Scented soft plastics such as Trigger-X baits on a ¼ ounce jig head are extremely productive and a lot of fun to fish. A live shrimp either free lined or fished under a cork is the top choice for anglers who prefer live bait. Fish will begin moving south from the passes to the flats between Stickney Pt. and Blackburn Pt. and will be scattered over a large area. Successful anglers will fish quickly until the fish are located.

Redfish schools will be thinning out in the shallow water, but there will still be plenty of fish in the pot holes, along mangrove shorelines, and around oyster bars. Rapala plugs, weedless gold spoons, and jigs are all excellent choices for probing the shallow flats. These same lures will also catch snook, along with speckled trout and jack crevelle. Snook will be migrating through these areas on their way to their winter haunts and will be feeding heavily. Points, bars, and docks with current are prime ambush spots for game fish. Large live shrimp are deadly when fished under docks, although it will not allow anglers to cover nearly as much water. Night fishing under lighted docks and bridges will also produce a lot of snook this month.

King mackerel, Spanish mackerel, false albacore, cobia, and sharks will bend rods and test drags in the inshore Gulf of Mexico, provided the severe fronts stay away. Point of Rocks on Siesta Key is a prime fall spot to either sight cast to breaking fish or troll plugs and spoons. Live bait will also produce, especially once fish are located. Live blue runners and threadfins slow trolled on a "stinger" rig will catch some very nice kings along with sharks. Drifting a live shrimp or small bait fish will catch plenty of Spanish and albies.

Casting lures and flies to breaking fish on light tackle is tremendous sport! This is great fun and really relatively uncomplicated. Rig a light spinning outfit with a two foot piece of 30 lb fluorocarbon and tie on a silver spoon, jig with a shad tail, or a plug. Ease into casting range as quietly as possible and you are in business. In most instances an aggressive retrieve will trigger a bite. Fly anglers will do well with an 8 or 9 weight rod and a floating or intermediate sink tip line. Small, white flies work well; either a Glass Minnow or D.T. Special are the most popular.

December

December is a month that can test an angler's ability to adapt to current conditions. Water quality will vary throughout the area as passing cold fronts churn up the Gulf of Mexico. The flats between Stickney Pt. and Blackburn Pt. will be more productive under these circumstances. After several days of nice weather, the water near the passes will clear and those areas will once again be good spots to fish. Creeks and canals will attract fish as water temperatures drop.

Often times the tides will be very low in the morning in December. This will move trout, pompano, and other species off of the flats and into the deeper channels. There simply is not enough water up on the flat for them to be comfortable. Bouncing a jig down the sides of channel edges can be very productive. As the tide rises, fish will move up onto the flats to feed. Afternoon high tides can be the best time to fish the deep flats this time of year. A live shrimp under a cork is very effective, as are jigs with plastic grub tails. Natural colors such as olive, rootbeer, and motor oil work well in the slightly darker water.

Oyster bars south of Siesta Drive will hold redfish, snook, and trout, along with the first of the migrating sheepshead. Bars that drop off sharply into deeper water will be the most productive spots. Free lined live shrimp and scented soft plastics on a 1/8 ounce jig head work well. Docks, canals, and creeks in this same area will also hold fish, especially after fronts; the water will be warmer and cleaner in these areas. On cold mornings the very back of a canal will have the warmest and may concentrate fish.

There are several creeks and countless canals in our area, and all of them are productive winter time spots. Hudson Bayou, Whittaker Bayou, Bowles Creek, Phillippi Creek, South Creek, and the Grand Canal on Siesta Key are some of the most popular fishing holes. Rapala X-Raps work very well on snook and jack crevalle for anglers who prefer to cast artificial baits. They elicit explosive strikes and allow anglers to cover a lot of area fairly quickly. Once fish are located, large live shrimp and slowly worked soft plastic baits will also catch their share. Sheepshead and black drum will be found in the deeper holes, a live shrimp works best for these tasty bottom dwellers. Flounder seem to be plentiful this year and should also be caught in these areas.

Both Big Pass and New Pass will be good spots to fish when the water is clean, especially on the morning incoming tide. Jigs bounced off the bottom will catch pompano, bluefish, Spanish mackerel, and ladyfish. Keep moving until fish are located, then concentrate on that area making short drifts and motoring back around up-tide and drifting through again. Structure in both passes will attract sheepshead, along with grouper, snapper, flounder, and other species. Slack tides are the best times to fish these spots, a swiftly moving tide makes getting the bait to the bottom difficult. The many docks along Bird Key are especially productive for sheepies.

If the weather cooperates, Spanish mackerel and false albacore (bonita) should still be off of our beaches. Schools of game fish will be seen ravaging helpless bait fish on the surface. Silver spoons, plugs, and jigs cast into the melee' will all produce explosive strikes. This is a great opportunity to fly fishermen to experience some world-class fishing. A false albacore on a 9 weight rod is terrific sport!

Sarasota Species

Snook

Snook are southwest Florida's premier gamefish. They are elusive, grow quite large, will take live and artificial baits along with flies. Snook can be caught all year long; in the rivers and creeks in winter, the flats and bays in spring and fall, and the passes and beaches in the summer. Night fishing can be productive year-round. Plugs will elicit explosive strikes, particularly during low-light periods. Chumming with live pilchards in the warmer months will produce the best during the day. Live shrimp, jigs, spoons, and pinfish will also catch fish. They are fantastic table fare, but have a very limited harvest; most guides encourage catch-and-release.

Redfish

Redfish are another challenging and highly sought species in Suncoast waters. They are known in other parts of the country as "red drum" and "channel bass". Reds are caught all year long in the shallow water of the inshore bays, under docks, and around oyster bars. In late summer they school up in large numbers and move out into the Gulf of Mexico to spawn.   A large, live shrimp is a tough bait to beat, but pinfish, pilchards, and lures suck as jigs and spoons will also fool them.   Redfish are excellent table fare and have come back from severe over-fishing in the late 80's.

Spotted Sea Trout

Also known locally as "speckled trout", these are arguably the most popular inshore fish. They are plentiful cooperative, beautiful, and taste great and range along the entire Gulf Coast as well as up the mid-Atlantic. Trout are fairly aggressive and school up, so once fish are located the action can be non-stop. Jigs, plugs, flies, and live bait are all effective at catching speckled trout. They are available year round on the flats but will seek deeper holes in creeks and canals if it gets too cold. Larger trout (over 20") should be released unharmed as they are breeder females; the smaller trout make better table fare.

Tarpon

The "silver kings" invade the Suncoast from late winter in the southern region to May at the northern extremes on their annual spawning migration. These giants are the ultimate angling challenge and can be targeted using a variety of techniques. Live bait such as crabs and bait fish account for most of the tarpon hooked, though lures and flies will also fool some fish. Some resident and juvenile fish can be caught in certain areas all year long. Tarpon have no food value and there is no reason to kill one.

Spanish mackerel

"Spanny macks" are a terrific gamefish, providing anglers with action, great battles, and excellent table fare when eaten fresh. They are voracious feeders and will attack a fast moving lure or fly with reckless abandon. Live bait will catch plenty of fish, too. They prefer water temperatures in the high 60's to 80 degrees and are most numerous in the spring and again in the fall as they follow the baitfish migrations. Huge schools can be seen feeding on the surface in both the Gulf of Mexico and inshore bays.

Pompano

Very few fish get the locals as excited as do pompano. While they fish as hard as a fish three times its size, the incredibly delicious flesh is the attraction. Pompano are fantastic eating? These smaller cousins to the permit are caught in the passes, over the grass flats, and off of the beaches. Small jigs, live shrimp, and sand fleas are the top baits. Often times the fish can be seen "skipping" on the surface as a boat drives over them, giving away their location. They bunch up, once a pompano is hooked, that area should be worked thoroughly.

Mangrove snapper

Fishing for "mangs" has been outstanding over the last few years. These tasty saltwater panfish are normally caught around structure such as docks, bridges, and oyster bars. But, in recent years large numbers are being caught on the deep grass flats in open water. While snapper will occasionally take a lure, the vast majority are caught using live or frozen bait; shrimp and other baitfish. 15" is a nice fish for inshore water but they do grow to over ten pounds well offshore.

Bluefish

Bluefish are well known to anglers who fish the Atlantic coast. Here in Florida, they do not grow as large but are hard-fighting, vicious gamefish. Lures catch a lot of fish as they are attracted to fast moving baits, but live bait will also produce blues. They are found both inshore and in the Gulf, preferring areas of high salinity. Blues usually school up, so once they are located it is usually "Game on!" While bluefish are edible, they are strong and less desirable than many other species caught locally. Enjoy the battle and let them go to please another angler.

Jack crevelle

Jacks are aggressive, hard fighting fish that are found year round in Florida and provide great sport on light tackle. They range from hand-sized fish up to twenty-plus pound bruisers. There is no finesse with these guys; they just pull until they can't pull any longer. They will hit almost any lure or bait, the key is finding them. Jacks are normally schooled up in tight bunches and are quite competitive, resulting in an aggressive strike. They have strong, dark meat and are not considered good to eat.

Flounder

Most of the flounder caught on the Suncoast are Florida Gulf flounder, which do not grow as large as their Atlantic cousins. They are often found near structure such as docks, bridges, and artificial reefs. They are also caught on the grass flats, usually lying in holes or along drop-offs, waiting to ambush a meal. Flounder hang very close to the bottom, so that is where the bait or lure needs to be. They will hit most live baits and a slowly bouncing jig will catch fish, too. Flounder are at the top of many anglers list when it comes to good eating!

Sheepshead

Sheepshead are an unusual looking fish, easily distinguished by its vertical black stripes and human-looking teeth. They will almost always be found near some type of submerged structure, eating crabs, barnacles, and other critters that live nearby. Very few are caught on lures and they are notorious as bait-stealers. Live shrimp, sand fleas, and fiddler crabs are the top baits. They fight hard and are most plentiful in winter and early spring. They taste great but are difficult to clean due to their large spines and tough rib bones.

Gag Grouper

While grouper are more known for being an offshore species, quite a few are caught inshore. They are structure-oriented and will be found near docks, bridges, rocks, and other structure with a little depth. Live bait fools most of them, though they will hit a jig or plug. In summer they school up and can be caught on the deep grass flats as they migrate out of the bays and into the Gulf. Grouper are prized table fare, but very few fish caught in the bay will be of legal size, but they are great sport on light tackle.

Black Sea Bass

These tasty little saltwater panfish do not get very big inshore, but boy are they fantastic eating! Most of the sea bass are caught accidently while fishing for other species. They readily hit jigs bounced near the bottom on the flats and in the passes. Live shrimp will also catch a lot of fish. Structure in the bays and artificial reefs just offshore will also hold fish.

Cobia

Cobia are a pelagic species (they migrate up the coast in the spring and back down in the fall) and are found over structure in the inshore Gulf of Mexico and on the flats inshore. Often times they can be seen swimming along right under the surface. They are curious fish and will readily take a well-presented lute and seldom turn down a large shrimp or pinfish. Cobia are great eating but must be 33" to the fork, so better to net them and not use a gaff unless you are sure they are legal. They are great fighters, but watch out for the row of spines on top.

Black Drum

Black drum are similar looking to sheepshead but are more closely related to redfish. They are structure-oriented bottom feeders that prefer shrimp and crabs to bait fish. Very few are caught using artificial lures. Some very large specimens will be found in shallow water near oyster bars and they bite fairly lightly for their size. Cooler months are generally best. The smaller drum are good eating but larger fish can get a bit wormy.

Ladyfish

Some anglers look down on ladyfish, but they have saved many a charter, especially on a cold winter day. They are aggressive and school up, so once located the action can be fast and furious. There is no need for live bait with these guys; jigs will catch all you want. They are also great sport on fly and a good fish to use to teach kids how to play a fish, as they almost always jump and make runs. They are available year round in the bays and inshore Gulf. They have no value as a food fish.

Fishing Spots in Sarasota

Here is a list of the top fishing spots in Sarasota. These are places that I fish almost every day, depending on the season and conditions. In order to limit redundancy, I will use the following terms when describing these spots.

THIS IS A GUIDE ONLY, DO NOT USE FOR NAVIGATION!

"Deep grass flats" are from 4' to 10' in depth and will hold speckled trout, Spanish mackerel, bluefish, pompano, jacks, grouper, snapper, sharks, flounder, and ladyfish.

"Shallow grass flats" are 3' or less and hold snook, redfish, larger trout, and jacks.

"Docks" will attract sheepshead, snook, redfish, drum, flounder, and snapper.

"Bars" are shallow bands of sand, usually with grass and/or oysters that drop off on one side into slightly deeper water. They attract snook, trout, reds, sheepshead, jacks, and more.

Most of these are large areas, not one specific spot.

1) Long Bar; a very long, shallow bar that nearly crosses the entire bay. Deep grass flats are found on the west end as well. Best on a low, incoming tide. A great spot to fish!

2) Buttonwood Harbor; a very large area of deep grass with a shoal (shallow flat) on the east end. Lush shallow abound near Longboat Key. Helicopter Shoal is a long, narrow bar several hundred yards to the south. A deeper channel runs into the basin and is a good winter spot. Another VERY good year-round spot.

3) Bowlees Creek; deep grass surround the mouth of Bowlees Creek and spoil islands and bars line the channel itself. The east side of the bay in both directions has shallow grass flats that drop off and will hold fish at times.

4) Bishop's Point; easily distinguished by four large condominiums, Bishop's Point is a classic point that starts shallow and slowly tapers off into deeper water. Excellent deep grass flats exist on both sides while an excellent shallow flat lies between the bar and the shoreline.

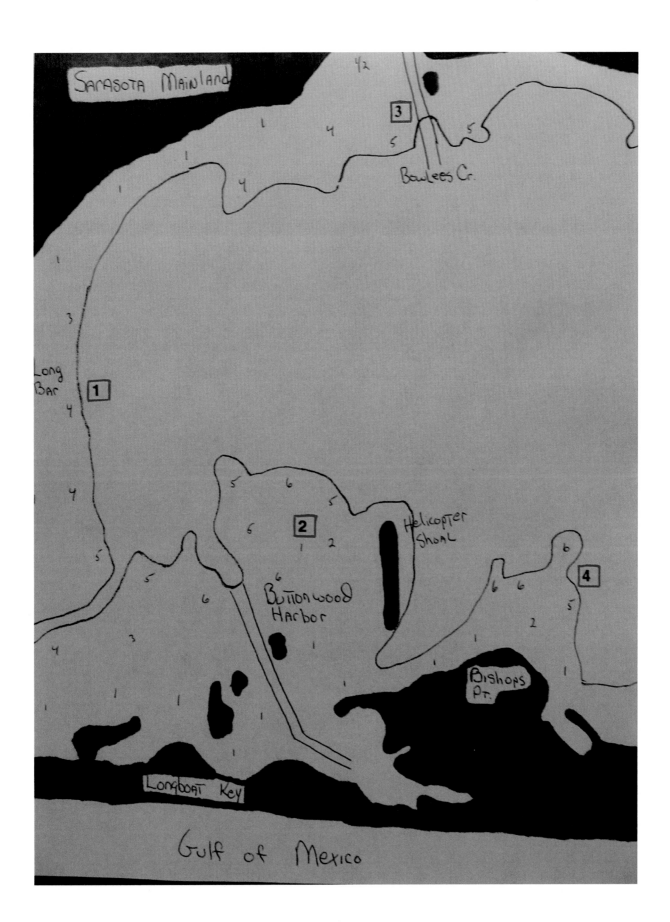

5) Stephen's Point/Ringling flats; this is a great spot, particularly for speckled trout. An underwater "hump" exists a few hundred yards from shore with a lot of grass that holds bait and fish. Bars along the shoreline from the Ringling Mansion north are good for snook and reds.

6) The east side of Sarasota Bay can be good, especially on a hard east wind. Shallow bars with grass and docks drop off into deeper water. Look for bait and birds. Residential canals along here will hold snook and jacks and are good spots on windy days.

7) Hart Reef; 27.22.015/82.34.574 concrete rubble placed in deeper water that holds grouper, snapper, tarpon and more.

8) Country Club Shores/Moorings; a large bar runs parallel to shore here, starting very shallow then dropping off into deeper water with grass growing to 10'. This area will hold a wide variety of species. An artificial reef lies at the north end of CC Shores.

9) Middlegrounds; a fantastic fishing spot! A large area of both deep and shallow grass close to the Gulf of Mexico that attracts just about every fish that swims. Trout, bluefish, pompano, mackerel, jacks, ladyfish, sharks, snapper, and even cobia will move into this area to feed.

10) New Pass; connects the Gulf and Sarasota Bay and can hold a lot of fish, particularly in spring and fall. Pompano, mackerel, ladyfish, blues and more will be caught in the pass. Structure such as docks and the bridge are good for sheepshead, snapper, and more. Docks on Ken Thompson Island and another park on the north side of the bridge are great places for anglers without a boat to fish.

11) Zwicks Channel; a deeper cut going north, it holds trout in the winter and docks are good year-round. Also a great place to catch white bait.

12) Radio Tower; a large area of submerged grass extending from the anchored sailboats south to the Ringling Causeway, this is another large area that is very productive for a variety of species. Pop Janzen Reef lies at the south end.

13) There is a deep channel that cuts through a shallow flat here and can be very good for trout and redfish. Docks along here also hold snook, reds, drum, and sheepshead. A good spot in winter and on a strong northwest wind.

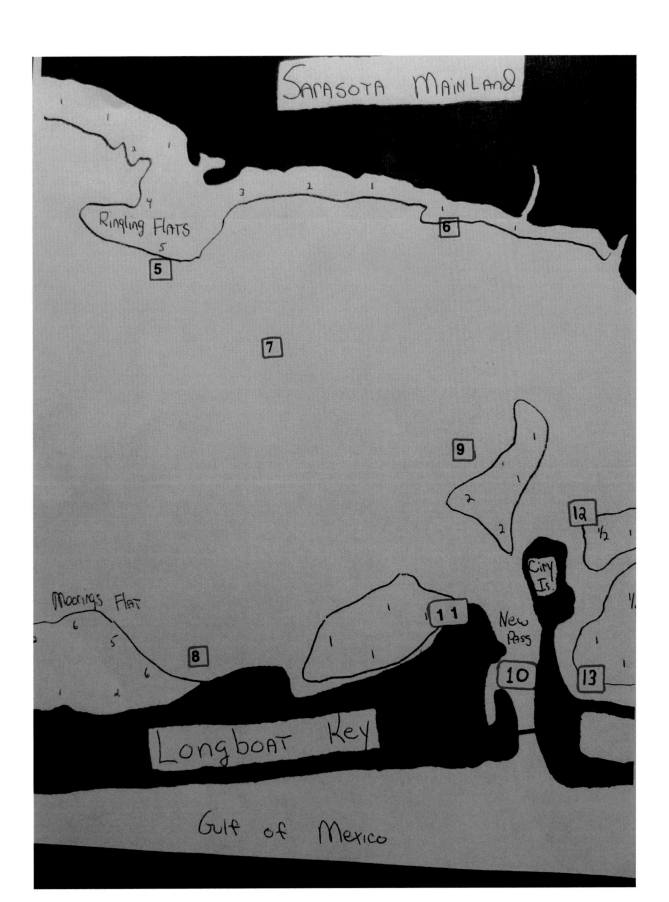

14) Bridges; the Ringling Bridge, "Twin Bridges", and Siesta Drive Bridge are all good spots to catch fish both day and night. Bay Island Park lies on the west side of the Siesta Drive Bridge and is a handy spot for anglers without a boat.

15) Marina Jacks; an area of submerged grass with a shallower crown just off of the anchored boats. Shallow flats to the south off of Selby Gardens are good for snook and reds, as is Hudson Bayou.

16) Marker #5; another good grass flat in 5' to 7' of water that holds a lot of fish at times. Speckled trout, Spanish mackerel, bluefish, pompano, ladyfish, and more will hit jigs and live bait.

17) Bird Key docks; Bird Key is man-made and the dredging required to do so results in deeper water surrounding the key. Docks line Bird Key and many will hold sheepshead, snapper, flounder, and other structure oriented species.

18) Otter Key; a deeper dredge area cuts through the keys here. Structure and holes abound and holds many species. The Yacht Club Channel can also be good when windy.

19) Big Pass; a veritable fish highway, Big Pass is a fantastic spot to fish! Pompano, mackerel, blues, and ladyfish will be found in the middle. Structure lines the north side of Siesta Key all the way out to the mouth and holds snook, sheepshead, snapper, reds, grouper, and drum.

20) South Lido Park; a great spot for shore-bound anglers, offering access to the Gulf and Big Pass. A nice grass flat lies to the southeast and is a great place to wade for trout. Be wary of strong tides, do NOT wade out near the point or in the channel!

21) Spoil Islands; spoil islands are the result of dredging the Intracoastal and can be great spots to fish. Snook, snapper, trout, reds, and more will hold here, especially when baitfish are abundant. Be careful of shallow water!

22) Skiers Island; grass flats in 4' to 6' of water surround the island, as well as nice oyster bars to the north. The Grand Canal is a good place to fish docks and to troll.

23) Bars and shallow grass good for trout, snook, and redfish.

24) Beaches; area beaches are probably the best bet for anglers fishing from shore. Whiting, silver trout, flounder, and sheepshead will take shrimp or a small jig in the winter. Spanish mackerel, ladyfish, bluefish, jacks, and more will be found in spring and fall. Sight fishing for snook can be fantastic in the summertime. Anglers in boats will catch mackerel, kings, false albacore, sharks, tarpon, and other species.

25) Field Club flat; an area of scattered grass in 4' to 6' of water, getting very shallow at the south end. Docks will hold fish as well.

26) Phillippi Creek; a VERY good place to fish in the cooler months. Jacks, snook, snapper, sheepshead, drum, and more will inhabit the creek. Live shrimp works well as does shallow diving plugs. Snook and jacks will migrate a long way up the creek if it gets cold.

27) This stretch of the Intracoastal has a lot of rocky ledges that are good for snapper and sheepshead.

28) Stickney Point; a park just south of the bridge offers access to shore-bound anglers. Fishing from the bridge itself is also permitted. Snook, ladyfish, jacks, and bottom fish are the main targets. Very good at night.

29) A nice little flat lies southeast of Stickney Point and will hold snook, redfish, and trout. The small creek is good as well, but is quite shallow.

30) Point of Rocks; the best beach spot in the area, offering great fishing when conditions are right but requiring a little walking as access is limited.

31) Nice bar and grass flat east of Marker # 51, good for trout.

32) Bars on both sides of the bat at Marker #50 are very good. Fish shallow for snook and reds and the deeper edges for speckled trout.

33) Vamo; nice shallow bars and grass with access to North Creek just to the south. There is a park that is a good place to wade or launch kayaks and canoes.

34) Neville Preserve; good grass with sharp drop-offs, fish will school up in the channel.

35) Flats and bars south of Spanish Point on both sides are good for a variety of species.

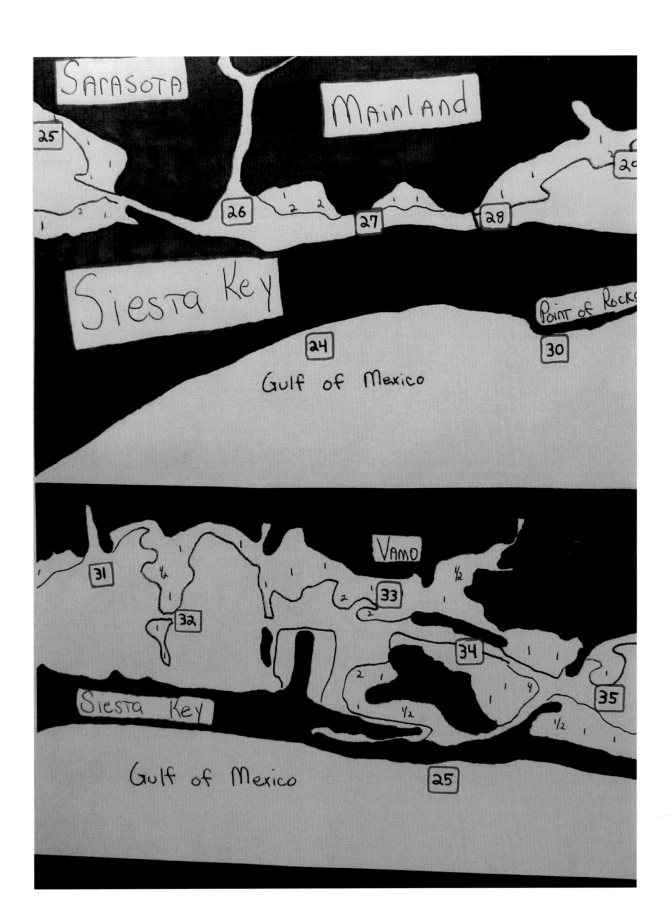

Made in the USA
Middletown, DE
27 July 2018